ASPERGER SYNDROME
and
ALCOHOL

ASPERGER SYNDROME and ALCOHOL

DRINKING TO COPE?

Matthew Tinsley and Sarah Hendrickx

Foreword by Temple Grandin

JESSICA KINGSLEY PUBLISHERS
LONDON AND PHILADELPHIA

First published in 2008
by Jessica Kingsley Publishers
116 Pentonville Road
London N1 9JB, UK
and
400 Market Street, Suite 400
Philadelphia, PA 19106, USA

www.jkp.com

Library of Congress Cataloging in Publication Data
Tinsley, Matthew.
 Asperger syndrome and alcohol drinking to cope? / Matthew Tinsley and Sarah
Hendrickx ; foreword by Temple Grandin.
  p. cm.
 Includes bibliographical references (p.   ) and index.
 ISBN 978-1-84310-609-8 (pb : alk. paper) 1. Asperger's syndrome--Patients-
-Alcohol use. 2. Dual diagnosis. I. Hendrickx, Sarah. II. Title.
 RC553.A88T56 2008
 362.29--dc22

                                                    2008002221

British Library Cataloguing in Publication Data
A CIP catalogue record for this book is available from the British Library

ISBN 978 1 84310 609 8

Printed and bound in Great Britain by
Athenaeum Press, Gateshead, Tyne and Wear

CONTENTS

FOREWORD

During my teens and twenties, I had horrible non-stop anxiety and panic attacks. Between the ages of 20 to 30, the panic episodes got worse. My nervous system was in a constant state of hyper vigilance. My brain was acting as if I was in a jungle filled with dangerous predators that would eat me. To get other people to understand how I felt, I often told teachers and journalists. Remember how you felt when you took final exams in college or remember how you felt when you were getting ready to interview a very important person? It was like having final exam "nerves" everyday. I was desperate for relief.

I came from the era where psychoanalysis was used. In my twenties I thought that if I could understand the deep dark secrets of my psyche, the "anxiety" would go away. No matter how much I searched for the secret source of my anxiety, it would not go away. Throughout my twenties I used my squeeze pressure machine to calm my anxiety, along with lots of exercise. The pressure machine is described in detail in Thinking in Pictures. Hard physical exercise done every day calmed my anxiety. My "anxiety" attacks became increasingly debilitating throughout my twenties, I got the sweats, sometimes I had difficulty swallowing, my heart would pound and my stomach did flip flops. I would break out in a sweat on the way to the mailbox because I was afraid I might get a "bad" letter. It was ridiculous. My biology was overreacting and treating something that should have been a minor annoyance as if a lion was stalking me.

Like Matthew Tinsley, I could have easily fallen into the trap of becoming dependent on alcohol. At important work social events I always used to have a few drinks because it calmed me down. To avoid having a problem, I never consumed alcohol in my house, but not everyone has the willpower to do this. Many people on the autism spectrum in fact go on to self medicate with other kinds of drugs.

Antidepressant medications started in my early thirties saved me from these possibilities. If I had not discovered the calming effects of antidepressants I could have easily become addicted to alcohol or drugs. I know many creative people who were either drug or alcohol addicts who have really been helped by fluoxetine (Prozac). When I first started taking an old fashioned antidepressant called immipramine (Tofranil), it made me a believer in biochemistry. Within three days, the horrible panic attacks were 90% gone. Two other friends I know who have autism have also been helped by Prozac to control nonstop anxiety and panic.

When medication is used, the doses often have to be lower for people on the autism/Asperger spectrum. Medication works best for anxiety when the person has full activation of the "fight or flight" nervous system for trivial reasons. There are calmer individuals, however, who do not have a nervous system that gets into a full panic easily. These individual do not usually need medication. Plenty of exercise and cognitive behavioral therapy should work well for them. Research clearly shows the benefits of vigorous exercise on anxiety. I also got great insight into my own condition by reading first person accounts of other people on the spectrum. That helped me greatly in my social life.

To deal with anxiety in my life, I had to work on it from three different angles – medication, exercise, and having interesting work that I can do with other people with similar interests. Being well-informed about the difficulties that people on the spectrum face is also very important. By spreading awareness of the potentially huge number of people on the spectrum who do in some way find themselves drinking to cope, Sarah Hendrickx and Matthew Tinsley are doing the AS community a huge service and will hopefully help others to avoid the same problems.

Temple Grandin,
author of Thinking in Pictures

INTRODUCTION

Alcohol and Asperger Syndrome: a dangerous combination or a successful coping strategy? For those who experience difficulty in interacting,
socializing or simply being in the presence of other people, the verbally,
socially and physically lubricating and loosening effects of alcohol can
provide a gateway into an otherwise impenetrable and overwhelming
arena where people mingle, make small talk and get to know each other.
Alcohol can maintain friendships, give access to a whole host of relationships and even sustain careers. But…what happens when the addictive
quality of the substance becomes more than just a handy tool to help one
get through the day? What happens when it threatens health and life and
the crutch becomes the very thing which destroys its user? What is the
individual left with, when the panacea is taken away?

This book seeks to question to what extent alcohol and Asperger
Syndrome (AS) meet each other. Part of the research for the book
involved contacting a number of specialists in the field of AS to enquire as
to their knowledge of any previous research that existed or of anything
related that was known to them. The overwhelming response was one
along the lines of: 'You're onto something; this is a piece of work that
needs doing. I've never seen any research and I have no idea where you
should start. Good luck!' – that kind of thing; encouraging in one way,
but daunting in another.

The premise on which this book was founded was Matt's experience
as a late diagnosed adult with an Autistic Spectrum Condition (ASC): Pervasive Developmental Disorder Not Otherwise Specified (PDD-NOS),
also known as Atypical Asperger Syndrome, or Atypical Autism, to be

precise. Matt went through life until the age of 43 as a constantly anxious man who managed his feelings of stress, panic and fear with an increasing amount of, initially, tranquillizers and, subsequently, alcohol. By doing so, Matt achieved a successful education, working life, relationships and independence. The collapse of this fairly successful coping strategy manifested as alcoholism and resulting serious illness. A period in hospital then rehabilitation ensued, with a subsequent diagnosis of an ASC. Matt now has a new, dry life with his ASC and without his alcohol.

I am a practitioner and trainer in Asperger Syndrome and have worked with many people with Asperger Syndrome and similar conditions on the Autistic Spectrum, who manage their daily lives in a variety of ways, often with great ingenuity and skill. I could see that Matt had been highly creative in finding something that for him enabled a life which met society's expectations of him – nothing short of genius. His life history is one of far greater success in terms of expected life goals (independence, career, relationships) than most individuals with an ASC I have encountered, all fuelled by alcohol. It worked for a long time before falling apart.

From our discussions, Matt and I felt that he could not be the only person who has managed life with undiagnosed AS by using an artificial means of controlling anxiety. In fact, it's a widely accepted means amongst the general population: 'Dutch Courage' we say, when we need to combat fear by knocking back a beer or two. 'Medicinal purposes', when we want to feel better with a brandy. The notion that alcohol helps us to cope is in our culture.

So, we decided to put a book together to see what information was available and to ask many more questions than we shall attempt to answer. We wanted to open up this possibility to alcohol services particularly: if a service user has AS, then the role that the alcohol plays in his or her life may be enormous, not easily removed and will need to be approached in a specific way. The theory-based and generalized elements of the book have been researched and written by me, with Matt contributing his personal account.

Matt also had a strong desire to 'give something back', as he feels that the knowledge of his AS and the support that he was given has not only changed his life, but saved his life. We hope that others may recognize themselves in his tale, have hope that it doesn't have to be this way, and that a different life is achievable. I didn't know Matt when he was drinking; I only know the calm, peaceful man who loves to share verbal banter, coffee (decaff for me, vente filter in a mug with room for milk for him), DVDs and Singapore noodles in our favourite haunt (he always has the Singapore noodles, and I always try to have something different, which I often end up hating, whilst he knows he is going to enjoy his choice – routine is a useful AS trait!). I think the determination he has shown to stay off the drink for over three years now, and the complete change he has made to his entire life have been nothing short of inspirational, and I'm so pleased he made it. If he hadn't made that choice and got the support he needed, there is no way he would still be here today to tell his tale.

We have attempted to gain a bigger picture of attitudes and behaviour regarding alcohol within the autistic community – regardless of whether individuals drink or not – but this has proved hard to achieve, as accessing willing participants is difficult. Some people are justifiably fed up of 'researchers' asking them questions, and ban such requests on their online forums. Alcohol services are also often ill-equipped to recognize possible AS. They are bound, rightly so, by confidentiality to discuss any service users that they may have suspicions of, and can in any case only give second-hand perspectives rather than the motivation and detail available from the people themselves. Also, we have a suspicion that many people do not know that they have AS because their drinking hides it and 'normalizes' them. These people have had no need for AS support or knowledge – so far. This factor is combined with the limited awareness and diagnosis of the condition amongst adults – reasons for which we shall discuss later. So, in short, the responses we received, whilst appreciated and valuable, are fewer than we would have liked.

Interestingly, I have undertaken similar work on the topic of sexual relationships and those with Asperger Syndrome for another book, and found people far more willing to discuss their sex lives than their drinking habits!

Those that have responded do not all have official diagnoses of AS; some are self-diagnosed. Given the difficulties and inconsistencies of adult diagnosis in the UK at this time, we have accepted their judgement without question. On occasion we have used the term 'ASC' (Autistic Spectrum Condition) as a catch-all for those with all autistic conditions including Kanner's/Classic Autism, Asperger Syndrome, High Functioning Autism, PDD-NOS, Semantic Pragmatic Disorder and any condition which affects individuals in a similar manner. While this term is used in order not to exclude any group, the expectation is that most people affected by alcohol will be those with free access to it – those not affected/less affected by an intellectual learning disability and who have independence regarding their consumption choices. This is more likely to be those with Asperger Syndrome than Classic Autism, for example. Hence we have settled on 'AS' as the most common term for those that the book is intended to examine.

We would like to thank those people for their time and their honesty and hope that this book helps to increase understanding of their perspectives and experiences.

The book does not focus on drug misuse. We acknowledge that there are suggestions that marijuana use may be prevalent within the AS population as a similar means of anxiety management. The motivation is pretty much the same; just the medication is different. There is the added complication of illegality with drug use, which makes it even harder to document, as people are less likely to disclose their usage honestly. Alcohol is a legal, socially acceptable, everyday substance which is easily accessible. The concepts, motivations and treatment strategies for alcohol can be transposed to drug misuse to some degree, so we feel that there is some relevance for those working in related fields.

We hope that this book will provide further awareness of AS and the impact and consequences that it can have for an individual. This book is the first extensive look into the overlap between these two conditions and as such brings with it little data, evidence or previous research. This makes it a tentative initial enquiry into a new area. We cannot conclude that there is a link, due to lack of evidence, but will attempt to present the mitigating factors of both conditions and consider where their overlap lies. We hope that we have opened the door for further research and discussion that we did not have the resources to engage in. Most of all we hope that we can alert those working on the ground to keep an eye out for what may be a hidden epidemic.

I can remember with great clarity the first time that Asperger Syndrome impinged on my consciousness. After a successful 20-year career working in specialist bookshops I was unemployed, with a failed marriage and living with my mother. I was also a chronic alcoholic.

This particular morning I was reading a newspaper over breakfast (a half-bottle of gin to keep alcohol withdrawal symptoms at bay), when an interview with Mark Haddon about his book *The Curious Incident of the Dog in the Night-time* came on the television. I was absent-mindedly listening when the litany of key indicators of the syndrome struck me as being very familiar. Love of routine, a phenomenal memory, great clumsiness and lack of common sense were the four which sent me immediately to the internet to try and find out more about the condition.

The more I read, the more excited I became. At last I felt a hope that I would begin to understand why I was like I was: that I would be finally able to 'get' myself. However, at this time I was in the final few months of active alcoholism, which would leave me hospitalized twice and very nearly dead. Luckily, I chose to attend a wonderful rehabilitation centre, which gave me the time, space and opportunity to find out more about who I was and why exactly I had experienced the life I had up until that point.

On leaving rehab, I chose to go to Brighton to study, and to my eternal good fortune I met Sarah, someone with whom I could share a common interest in this condition, as well as a great friendship.

It was at her gentle suggestion that I began to join her in delivering talks to professionals about my experiences. She firmly believed that others might be interested in hearing about my perspective on both life with AS, and as a recovering alcoholic, whose continuing recovery was based as much on self-knowledge as someone on the Autistic Spectrum, as it was on the therapy I had received in rehab.

I found that many people were greatly interested in hearing not only Sarah's expert training on the background of AS and strategies to help those with it, but also my personal view of what I had done to lead a relatively 'normal' life, what it had led to and how I cope today.

I had vaguely considered writing about my life whilst in rehab, but it was the jolt of meeting others with the condition, as well as seeing how useful many people had found the talks that Sarah and I gave, which was the real spur to putting together a book on the subject. I was very aware of how I deal with everyday life, using my self-knowledge as a coping tool instead of turning to alcohol and tranquillizers as I had done so often in the past. If anything that I have gone through could be put to good use in order to help others in my situation, then I saw it as my duty to disseminate the information to as wide an audience as possible.

I find that I am now leading a truly happy life, with no need for artificial calmatives, and am grateful for the opportunity I have been given to see life as it really is, and not through the distorted window that alcohol gave me. It is my hope, and Sarah's, that others in a similar predicament to me will find our experience and suggestions useful in finding a better way to live, and to be.

CHAPTER 1

ASPERGER SYNDROME AND ALCOHOL - WHY SHOULD THERE BE A LINK?

In order to understand what we are dealing with, it is useful to outline some basic terms of reference. We shall look at alcohol usage, what defines alcoholism and other concepts. We shall also look at what aspects of AS may cause a person to be drawn to alcohol and what the subsequent effects may be. There have been a number of studies on people with alcoholic disorders which focus on their information processing and experience of symptoms of social anxiety. Some of this work is mentioned in this chapter, but is only a small sample of what exists in this field.

Academic professionals and clinicians contacted during the compilation of this book all agreed that, for some, alcohol is used as a means of managing AS, but none had any advice on where to find the evidence for this, because there do not seem to be any studies – clinical or otherwise – on this topic. Some writers, such as Berney and Tantam, make passing mention of high numbers of those with AS who are alcoholics, but don't elaborate as to the details of these statements. Anecdotally, in personal communication with workers in AS and alcohol support, it is not unusual to hear sentiments such as, 'Most people with drink problems probably have Asperger Syndrome', although when probing further to locate the source of this supposition, it just seems to be accepted as a given. It is one of those things that some people in the field just seem to 'know' or assume. Research into this topic would be enormously difficult and presumably this is why no one has tried to uncover the real picture. We have presented some examples of studies into related areas where appropriate. Obstacles in the path of revealing the nature and extent of the issue may include:

- Wide-spread lack of adult diagnosis of AS: many adults do not have diagnoses due to the relatively recent discovery of the condition. Those that are self-diagnosed may not be eligible to participate in research.

- Many individuals being unaware of their own AS: many people may not know that they have AS, especially those who are older and who have just accepted or overcome their differences, perhaps by self-medicating with alcohol.

- Lack of knowledge of AS by service providers: alcohol, GP or other support services may not 'spot' someone displaying AS characteristics, and therefore not provide access to diagnosis or specific support.

- Hiding known AS: some people may feel that they do not want to disclose their autism for fear of consequences in the workplace or in life in general.

- Stigma in admitting to a mental health issue (e.g. anxiety or depression) that may lead on to diagnosis of AS due to the large degree of overlap (co-morbidity). There may be fear of exclusion, disbelief or negative consequences.

- Alcohol masking AS difficulties: the person may be very successful at hiding his or her AS characteristics with the use of alcohol, and again not be identified as a person needing support, or a person coping with anxiety.

- Lack of recognition of a drink problem: the person may not wish to disclose him- or herself as someone with a drink problem, or may not have come to this personal realization.

- Differences in cultural norms and behaviours across countries and societies regarding alcohol (and what constitutes 'a problem'), which may make direct comparisons difficult.

- Differences in cultural norms and behaviours across countries and societies regarding identification diagnosis of AS, which may make direct comparisons difficult.

- A strategy which began as a simple coping behaviour (drinking to increase confidence) shifting into an addiction (for the substance itself, rather than its effects), at which point it is hard to separate the original motives from the end result.

- Measuring levels of ability after the onset of alcoholism, which makes it difficult to assess pre-alcoholism ability levels and thus ascertain the extent of the effect of drinking. Assumptions may be made that pre-alcoholism performance levels were in the 'normal' range, when in fact they were not.

Why alcohol?

Why do people choose to drink alcohol? It seems that there are many answers to this question.

- People drink to be part of a social group or to change their mood; to gain acceptance; to forget reality; to feel carefree and brave; to feel less anxious and afraid; and for many other reasons.

- The physiological effects of alcohol on the brain involve the suppression of the parts which are associated with social inhibition. In simple terms, alcohol helps to stop one from worrying so much about doing or saying the wrong thing.

- Alcohol is easily available (in most countries).

- Many people with AS are extremely law-abiding and would not contemplate breaking the law. They would therefore choose a coping method that is legal in preference to illegal substances.

- Finding illegal substances may require social contacts and skills and a degree of tact and subtlety that someone with AS may not have. Buying alcohol does not.

- Alcohol is widely known, used and accepted as a social relaxant (in many cultures).

- Alcohol is relatively cheap. Many people with AS are un- or under-employed and on a low income. It is an affordable drug.

- Drinking is not only socially acceptable; it is socially expected. Those who do not drink are sometimes seen as strange. Therefore, drinking is a way of acceptance and sign of 'normal' behaviour. The attitude of society towards those who choose not to drink is often that they have some kind of problem for not joining in.

- There is a strong media portrayal, on TV and in films, of groups of people (friends) having a good time in pubs and bars, which are seen as the places to go to have friends, meet partners and socialize. The effect may be that a person who would like friends and a social network may believe that this is the only way to achieve these.

- The effects are almost immediate.

- It seems to allow easier emotional expression. People who are drunk tend to exhibit extremes of emotions – happiness, sadness and anger – to a greater degree than when sober.

- Alcohol seems to numb anxiety and lift mood (albeit, arguably, temporarily).

- For some, alcohol seems to make unpalatable activities more tolerable.

Alcoholism – a definition

It is estimated that around 12 per cent of men and 3 per cent of women are dependent on alcohol, which is around 3.8 million people in the UK. Around 90 per cent of people drink alcohol at least occasionally, and the cost of government-funded hospital services paying for alcohol related illness is estimated at up to £3 billion per year (Addaction 2008).

Around 73 per cent of men and 60 per cent of women in the UK drank in the week prior to being asked for a major alcohol survey (The Information Centre 2007), so we can see that drinking alcohol is more typical that not drinking at all. Drinking in itself is not a problem as it is accepted and even expected, but a fine line exists between enjoying a drink and needing a drink.

There is much debate and confusion around the definition of what constitutes an 'alcoholic', and whether this is a different state than that of a 'problem drinker' or the same thing by any other name. Drinking alcohol to the extent that it causes the user problems does not, for some writers, make an alcoholic. Defining 'excess' or even 'problems' is highly subjective and will depend on culture, personal viewpoint and any number of other factors. If you do not drink at all yourself, you are more likely to measure the consumption of someone else differently than if you are a regular drinker. Similarly, drinking two–three pints at lunchtime may be a workplace norm for some, and yet look like an addiction to others. Goodwin (2000, p.31) stresses that the difference between the problem drinker and the alcoholic is 'a vulnerability to alcohol that sets him (the alcoholic) apart from other drinkers'. Quantity or type of alcohol consumed is also not a reliable measure of the extent of a person's issue as this can be misleading due to personal tolerance and patterns of consumption.

The labelling of a person as someone with alcoholism or a drink problem is only useful in gaining access to appropriate services and ensuring that treatment and support are designed on an individual basis to meet the needs of the person. It is useful, however, to try and establish what defines a 'problem'.

Royce and Scratchley (1996) define alcoholism as 'a chronic primary illness or disorder characterized by some loss of control over drinking, with habituation or addiction to the drug alcohol, or causing interference in any major life function, for example: health, job, family, friends, legal or spiritual'. They also discuss the concept of primary and secondary alcoholism, which may be a useful distinction for those with AS. Primary alcoholism is described as being where the alcoholism is the basic condition requiring treatment, regardless of the cause. Secondary alcoholism is where the alcoholism is a symptom of another condition. This is also described as reactive alcoholism. This may apply to some with AS, as their drinking is a result of trying to manage their underlying autism, rather than for other reasons. It is vital that the possibility of the alcoholism being a reactive agent be considered when working with alcoholics. If there is a need for the alcohol to perform an essential function, then its removal will expose all of those needs and perhaps reveal the extent of the person's autism for the first time. Support is required for this process.

For the purposes of this work we choose to ignore the distinction between the two, and therefore define problem drinking and alcoholism as the experience of significant problems caused by drinking alcohol, and the continuation of the drinking, regardless. It relates to an inability and/or refusal to stop the behaviour which is leading to the problems experienced.

Autistic Spectrum Conditions – a social difference

In order to get a picture of the other side of the equation, let's look at the features and characteristics of AS and explore those that specifically may lead a person to drink.

The Autistic Spectrum is a range of developmental conditions that all impact in the same areas of a person's ability but in a multitude of different ways, which varies from individual to individual. The spectrum ranges across intelligence levels from those with a learning disability (Classic Autism) to those without (Asperger Syndrome, PDD-NOS). We are looking at those at the end of the spectrum which generally does not include a learning disability (Asperger Syndrome), purely because those with a learning disability are more likely to be supported in daily living and have less unsupervised access to alcohol. AS is a life-long, probably genetic, condition that affects how the individual communicates and interacts with the external world. The difficulties that a person with AS experiences are spread across all areas of life which involve other people and the external environment: the social world, managing change, planning and organization and understanding non-verbal language, to mention just a few. For many, it is other people and their expectations that are often the biggest problem. To someone with AS, people are often confusing, contradictory, unpredictable and irrational. Unfortunately, communicating and dealing with people is an unavoidable facet of life for most of us. Similarly, it is impossible to manage and control all contact with sensory and environmental sources, which may also cause stress responses to those who experience sensitivity to external factors.

> This is so difficult. I don't know what to do, when, where or why. Sometimes I wish people wouldn't try to engage me and would just leave me alone. It would make my life so much simpler. (Male with Asperger Syndrome)

The argument that we are putting forward here is that for some with AS, alcohol is used as a means of numbing sensitivity, and reducing both anxiety and the need for life to be on the individual's terms. This group lives with the constant knowledge that the world is an exhausting and baffling place in a way that others seem not to experience. For some, alcohol may allow a greater degree of flexibility and tolerance of people and their desires (as opposed to one's own being paramount, which typifies the condition). Matt discusses this later when he writes about being married, and the demands of working life. He found he needed to drink in order to compromise his own wants and needs for those of others so that he could do what was required of him.

It is worth noting that there are currently likely to be many adults who have AS but have no diagnosis and may be unaware that they are affected by the condition. The work of Hans Asperger was not translated into English and given a name (Asperger Syndrome) until relatively recently, and so only younger people are likely to have had the benefit of early diagnosis and support. This adds to the complications of getting a realistic picture of how many people with AS are currently self-medicating (perhaps successfully) with alcohol or drugs. Some of these people may have come to the attention of mental health or substance misuse services, but due to a lack of knowledge of AS in many service providers may be labelled as having social anxiety or depression, or may simply be seen as alcoholics.

It is our belief that those with AS drink for the same reasons as many other problem drinkers and alcoholics, but with a different degree of necessity. Many people report using alcohol to deal with periods of anxiety, but this group drinks to combat high levels of anxiety which haunt them every moment of every day. Socializing is difficult for many people and many use alcohol to aid the process, but for those who have learned that the only way to avoid isolation and loneliness is to engage in a social marketplace which has rules, signs and language that you cannot read and do not understand, alcohol may be the only way to cope. Interestingly, those people with AS who did not drink, when asked how they cope with social situations, said that they simply avoided them. These people tended to be more isolated individuals who had no or few social relationships, and who suffered from feelings of depression and hopelessness as well as anxiety.

> I deal with anxiety by withdrawing into silence and backing out of social commitments (in a panicky all-or-nothing way) without consultation or consideration for others. (Male with Asperger Syndrome)

> Avoid the situation. (Male with Asperger Syndrome)

Those, like Matt, who have relied upon alcohol as a means of coping with everyday life have been allowed access to the social world. They have used alcohol to become 'normal' and desensitized to their natural state. This has allowed them to remain in the social arena, find friends, partners and jobs. It has allowed them to practise their social skills and become more adept at fitting in and learning how to behave. Many of those with AS who avoid social situations never gain this access and never vastly improve their social skills. Thus, alcohol works as a numbing device which enables tolerance, integration, acceptance and flexibility, which the person with AS may not naturally possess. It works, but only up to a point, after which it becomes potentially life-threatening. More of that later.

Temple Grandin, a renowned female writer and professor who has High Functioning Autism, recalls that she first drank alcohol in her late 20s at her parents' home. She drank half a glass of whisky and was shocked to realize how easy it would be for her to become dependent, so she stopped (personal communication, 2007). The all-or-nothing mindset of people with AS may make it harder for them to moderate their drinking in some cases, as they find it difficult to do anything in degrees. One man with Asperger Syndrome describes this:

> I find a small amount of alcohol stimulating and beneficial... I have difficulty, presumably because of the alcoholism, in curtailing consumption at the point of benefit... As this alcoholic drinking continues, the initial benefits are left behind and I become a drunken pain in the arse who still wishes more alcohol. (Male with Asperger Syndrome)

AS is characterized diagnostically by significant differences or deficits in social interaction, communication and language, and flexibility of thought and behaviour. Environmental sensitivity, although not mentioned specifically in the various diagnostic criteria for AS, is often said to feature as a factor for the majority of those with this condition. Those who completed questionnaires with regard to their drinking habits were asked what the main effects of having AS on them were. What follows is a selection of responses illustrating the diversity of the condition beneath the umbrella terms of the diagnostic criteria.

> Poor interaction with people, leading to social isolation, depression, lethargy and lack of ambition. (Male with Asperger Syndrome)

> Life-long difficulty making sense of what people get up to in their everyday lives and careers. Solitary habits...persistent and obsessive involvement in my own troubles and concerns. (Male with Asperger Syndrome)

> I can be aloof if I am worried that people do not want me to interact with them. I find it hard to cope with unpredictability. (Female with Asperger Syndrome)

> He doesn't like large social gatherings...finds it difficult to figure why other people think as they do, has tantrums... (Wife of male with Asperger Syndrome)

> Mental exhaustion trying to figure out life, relationships and social dynamics and consequences; three mental breakdowns, two in the past five years. Life-long depressive behaviour. (Male with Asperger Syndrome)

> Difficult to say. I tend to be my own person, but have problems of stress and anxiety fairly frequently. (Male with Asperger Syndrome)

Ultimately, breakdown of my marriage and abandonment of my professional life. (Male with Asperger Syndrome)

Further examples of the ways in which a person with AS may exhibit differences or deficits in these specific areas are as follows:

Social interaction

- Differences in the ability to read social cues, which others seem to know intuitively.

- A tendency to appear naïve, tactless or stupid by saying or doing the 'wrong' thing socially.

- Difficulty appreciating that the thoughts, feelings and opinions of other people are potentially different to one's own.

- A failure to adhere to social rules which often results in ridicule, aggression or exclusion.

People with AS may typically appear to be awkward in social situations, not picking up on unspoken 'rules'. They may behave in a socially inappropriate way, and find it hard to understand why their behaviour has offended or bothered others. For example, someone might mention how much weight a female colleague has put on recently, or speak very loudly about a personal issue. He or she may not be able to consider that others may find sensitive topics uncomfortable, only being able to see the matter from his or her own viewpoint.

Communication and language

- Difficulty reading non-verbal signals, body language and facial expression.

- Difficulty understanding subtleties of humour, sub-text and non-literal meanings of spoken language.

- A tendency to need very precise instructions and a preference to not be overloaded with information.

- A failure at times to communicate accurately, resulting in misunderstanding, stress and exclusion.

People with AS may find the language and emotions on the face difficult to 'read'. They may struggle to make eye contact, finding it pointless or overwhelming. Their language may be very pedantic and literal, and they tend to communicate in a very precise manner. They may also require information to be presented to them in a similarly detailed and exact way in order for it to be understood. If the understanding is not there, the person may be paralysed and have no idea what to do or how to react. This can lead to feelings of inadequacy, stupidity and low confidence. Thinking tends to be logical, and decisions are based on rational thought rather than emotions or feelings.

Lack of flexibility in thought and behaviour

- A need for own routines and preferred ways of doing things.

- Limited interests and conversational topics.

- A dislike of change, variety, surprises and spontaneity.

- Rigid thought patterns, and a tendency to find new concepts, planning, consequences and abstract thought difficult.

- An inability to tolerate flexibility, which can be stressful, anxiety-provoking and create difficulties within social relationships as the person may be seen as selfish and uncaring of others' needs.

- Black-and-white thinking: a tendency to see only one or two options to any situation, and an all-or-nothing approach to life, with a difficulty perceiving other options or degrees.

Managing unpredictable situations or changes to routines can be very stress-provoking for people with AS. Due to their reduced ability to understand all of the social interactions around them, they may cling to safe, known situations and routines in order to maintain a sense of control and familiarity in a world which feels chaotic and illogical. This can result in a narrow focus in both thought and action, where the individual is unable to consider other perspectives or behaviours outside that which is already known. The person may, for example, insist on eating the same food every day, sit in the same seat on the bus and become agitated when this is not possible, and find it difficult to manage changes at work or home. The tendency towards black-and-white thinking may result in unrealistic choices and perspectives. For example, someone in a relationship may feel that the relationship must be perfect and that any disagreement is a sign that it is a failure and should therefore be abandoned. The ability to consider the other positive aspects of the relationship is less developed.

Environmental sensitivity

- A limited range of tolerance for certain noises, smells, textures, physical touch etc.

- A need of and strong preference for certain noises, smells, textures, physical touch etc.

- An inability to tolerate or do without certain stimuli, which can result in isolation and withdrawal from environmental stressors.

Environments which are too stressful may be avoided by people with AS, as the sensory input is just too overwhelming for them to manage. If avoidance is not an option (because it is the workplace, for example), other coping strategies may be put into place. Alcohol may be one of the options for managing this stress and confusion. For some, the effort of coping with a working environment that they find difficult means that there is no spare energy to manage a social life or outside activities as well, since the effects of any individual stressors tend to be cumulative. The remainder of the person's time is spent alone, 're-charging' from the day.

Awareness of one's differences in each of these areas – usually learned from the reactions of others – can cause anxiety, stress and depression. The desire to participate socially and not be alone may cause some to use alcohol as a means to combat the anxiety of navigating all of the above social minefields.

Asperger Syndrome and anxiety disorders

> It seems completely reasonable to me that a person with
> Asperger Syndrome should be depressed or anxious. There's a
> constant possibility of failing in large and small ways and also a
> constant lack of real recognition from others, creating a persis-
> tent sense of isolation or lack of identity. (Male with Asperger
> Syndrome)

Although anxiety is not part of the defining diagnostic criteria of AS, we
can see that the characteristics briefly outlined above can reasonably be
expected to cause high levels of anxiety, stress and depression in those
who experience them; but what about further evidence of a connection?

Tony Attwood, a leading authority on Asperger Syndrome, sees those
with Asperger Syndrome managing anxiety as an everyday part of their
lives, with some of them going on to develop anxiety disorders, including
social anxiety disorder. He suggests that current research shows that
around 65 per cent of adolescents with Asperger Syndrome have a secondary mood or affective disorder (such as depression or anxiety)
(Attwood 2006).

> Social phobia, or social anxiety disorder, would be expected to
> be relatively common for those with Asperger Syndrome, espe-
> cially in the teenage and adult years when they are more acutely
> aware of their confusion in social situations, of making social
> mistakes, and possibly suffering ridicule. (Attwood 2006, p.140)

Schneier *et al.* (2002) see an overlap between social anxiety and other
disorders that are marked by social inhibition. They name Asperger
Syndrome, autism and alcoholism as three of these, alongside depression,
eating disorders and social avoidance. Berney (2004) also cites a strong
predisposition for those with Asperger Syndrome to exhibit co-
morbidity with a range of anxiety states and conditions, including social
phobia, panic disorder, obsessive compulsive disorder and others.

> I'm anxious quite a lot. (Male with Asperger Syndrome)

> I am anxious all the time because I don't know what's going to
> happen. I have a lot of sensory hypersensitivities, which I cope
> with through sensory routines (similar to OCD or Tourette's). I

> find it hard to tell how I feel or what I want, so I make arbitrary decisions. I feel isolated in social situations. (Female with Asperger Syndrome)

> I have had panic attacks in the past when I was in unfamiliar places without a familiar person to make me feel normal. (Female with Asperger Syndrome)

Interestingly enough, social anxiety (sometimes known as social phobia) is sometimes said to first appear in adolescence, when young people become aware that they are 'on their own' socially and that their performance will have an impact on their ability to attract friends and partners. This is also often the time at which AS becomes particularly noticeable and difficult, as the safe environment of junior school is exchanged for the more complicated, variable and larger world of secondary education. Both coincide with the onset of puberty and other internal and external changes in the body.

Whilst not suggesting that AS and social anxiety disorders are the same thing, it may be that some people diagnosed with social anxiety may in fact have AS and that their social fears are not entirely unjustified. It is these feelings that may drive a person to turn to alcohol in an attempt to subdue them. Anxiety is a necessary characteristic for social anxiety disorder, but anxiety is not part of the diagnostic criteria for AS; it just happens to be a by-product for large numbers of those with this condition. People with AS may have a legitimate fear of social errors, as they may be aware that their skills in this area have let them down in the past.

Social anxiety disorder is a recognized condition and is included in diagnostic manuals, such as Diagnostic Statistical Manual IV (DSM-IV) (American Psychiatric Association 1994). It is different to AS in that it is not necessarily a life-long condition – its onset tends to be during teenage years – and does not necessarily affect an individual's innate communication and language processing. However, there can be similarities in outcome: isolation, anxiety, low self-esteem and avoidance of social situations. Ghaziuddin (2005) points out that the DSM-IV says that a diagnosis of social anxiety disorder should not be made if a pervasive developmental disorder (AS is described as such) is present. He suggests that this implies that the symptoms of social anxiety must thus already be symptoms of these developmental disorders. Both those with AS and those with social anxiety disorder will avoid social situations for fear of humiliation and/or embarrassment at 'getting it wrong'. One adult with Asperger Syndrome explains this:

> It's not so much 'getting it wrong' but a matter of accepting (or knowing) time after time that you don't know what to do and have no hope of 'getting it right', so it's easier not to bother. (Personal communication, 2007)

Features of social anxiety disorder include:

- fear or anxiety in relation to people; being near, or having to interact with, others
- fear of judgement or criticism by other people, which may result in being hyper-sensitive to comment from others
- dread and panic before certain situations, and potential re-playing or ruminating on the event afterwards
- physical symptoms such as shaking, nausea and raised heart rate.

A related condition known as Avoidant Personality Disorder (APD) shows significant overlaps with social anxiety, and opinion varies as to the difference between the two. The suggestion is that APD is more severe and hard to shift than social anxiety, with the focus being on faulty thought patterns rather than the anxiety itself. Some of the features of APD are:

- persistent feelings of tension and fear
- lack of self-esteem and feelings of inferiority and inadequacy
- fear of being criticised socially
- limited or restricted lifestyle due to a need to have physical security
- avoidance of contact with people in any context for fear of social failure, inadequacy or rejection.

Alcohol and cognitive processing

There are a number of studies on issues around cognitive processing in alcoholics, some of which are outlined below, with some people showing an impaired ability in this area. There is no mention of any of the participants of the research having AS, but there is also no mention of what their cognitive processing was like before they became alcoholics.

It cannot be ruled out that some of these individuals already had a difference in their ability to decode facial expressions and emotions before they began to drink. Perhaps they started to drink because of an impaired ability to relate to and understand the communication of others throughout their lives.

It is reported that alcohol causes damage to the frontal lobe area of the brain through its toxicity, and this is also an area known to show differences in those with ASC. That these studies show overlap or a tendency for some alcoholics to have AS is pure conjecture, but it is interesting that some of the characteristics seen in some alcoholics are those that are prevalent in people with AS. The following are just a few examples of some of the work that has been carried out studying the processing of non-verbal information in alcoholics:

- One study (Philippot *et al.* 1999) investigated the ability of alcoholics to decode emotional facial expressions in comparison to a control group. The study found that the alcoholic participants made more errors in reading the expressions, but were not aware of their mistakes or their impaired ability to perform well at this task. The study further suggests a model linking abnormal processing of social information, stress and alcohol abuse.

- In a further study regarding emotional information processing in alcoholics, the researchers conclude: 'Alcoholics are specifically impaired on emotional non-verbal behaviour information processing: they are slower to correctly identify an emotion' (Foisy *et al.* 2007).

- Research examining theory of mind, humour processing and executive functioning – all areas which affect those with AS – in alcoholics found similar results (Uekermann *et al.* 2007).

The findings indicate that the alcoholic participants showed humour processing deficits which were related to theory of mind and executive functioning. They note that these deficits may contribute to interpersonal problems.

- Another study found that alcoholics had impairments in their ability to recognize correct prosody (the intonation and rhythm of speech which dictate meaning) and also in matching prosody to facial expression (Uekermann *et al.* 2005).

Alcohol and social anxiety

- The Mental Health Foundation compiled a comprehensive report on the relationship between alcohol and mental health (*Cheers? Understanding the Relationship between Alcohol and Mental Health*). They claim that 'the co-existence of alcohol problems and mental ill-health is very common' and that 'the idea that people "self-medicate" their mental health problems using alcohol is also very well known and well documented' (Mental Health Foundation 2006, p.5).

- The above study also states: 'The reasons we drink and the consequences of excessive drinking are intimately linked with our mental health, and this holds the key to dealing with growing worries about alcohol abuse' (Mental Health Foundation 2006, p.5).

- One study on alcohol use and social anxiety (phobia) states that the prevalence of problematic alcohol use amongst individuals with social phobia, as well as the prevalence of social phobia amongst those with alcohol problems, is more than would be expected by chance' (Abrams *et al.* 2002).

- A study of people meeting the DSM diagnostic criteria for social phobia examined the difference between those with and without alcoholism (Schneier *et al.* 1989). Those with alcoholism had more severe social phobia than the non-alcoholic group and were less likely to be married. The symptoms of social phobia were present before the alcoholism in 15 out of 16 cases, and most of these people said that they used alcohol to self-medicate their socially phobic symptoms. The study concludes that: 'Social phobia can be an important factor in the development of alcoholism' (Schneier *et al.* 1989, p.15).

- Research examining the use of alcohol as self-medication showed that those with social anxiety drank more prior to embarking on anxiety-provoking activities (public speaking) as opposed to more neutral tasks (reading silently) (Abrams *et al.* 2002).

- When extrapolating findings from a survey to the general population, it is estimated that up to 12 million adults in the UK drink to aid relaxation or overcome depressed feelings (Mental Health Foundation 2006).

- The *Cheers?* survey found that 'anxious people use drinking "to cope"' and are more likely to avoid social situations where alcohol is not available' (Mental Health Foundation 2006, p.7).

- Forty per cent of the *Cheers?* survey sample said that alcohol makes them feel less anxious. Those who say that alcohol helps with anxiety or depression are those who drink almost every day, and say they would have difficulty in stopping drinking (Mental Health Foundation 2006).

- The prevalence level of alcoholism within those who have social anxiety disorder is in the region of 20 per cent. In the general population, the level of alcoholism is around 10 per cent (Thomas, Randall and Carrigan 2003). Thus, those with social anxiety are twice as likely to become alcoholics as the general population.

Asperger Syndrome and alcohol – the link

The idea that alcohol reduces anxiety has been around since the 1950s, when Conger proposed 'tension reduction theory' (1956). Since then, much work has been carried out to develop this idea, and the consensus seems to be that alcohol does reduce tension for some people. Further work concluded that those that it did work for had high levels of social anxiety (Young, Oei and Knight 1990), although this was very much dependent on a number of other variable factors. The avoidance of social situations or use of self-medication (alcohol) to manage these events is well documented in social anxiety.

- One study focusing on the possible existence of a link between autism and addiction tentatively suggested that the two may have some common factors which predispose those with AS to addiction (van Wijngaarden-Cremers and van der Gaag 2006).

- 'Alcohol is an effective tranquillizer, particularly for someone who finds social groups uncomfortable. Asperger syndrome can add a compulsive quality to social drinking and encourage isolated drinking ungoverned by normal social conventions' (Berney 2004, p.346).

- AS is known to come with a range of co-morbid mental health conditions – depression, anxiety and alcoholism – according to Tantam (in Berney 2004), but the evidence is anecdotal rather than clinical, and thus so far tenuous.

- The historian Gilman Ostrander, quoted in *Alcoholism: The Facts* (Goodwin 2000), has a theory of alcoholism which proposes that it is a condition for individualists and loners. He states that it affects those who get a sense early in their lives that they are alone in the world. He believes that this prevents them from gaining emotional release through relationships with others, and leads to their finding this through alcohol. This would certainly fit the life experience of a person with AS, but for different core reasons.

- There is a high level of co-morbidity between AS and mental health problems, and mood disorders such as anxiety and depression.

- There are also high levels of co-morbidity between anxiety and admittance to alcohol rehabilitation units, with around 65 per cent of those admitted demonstrating both conditions (Mental Health Foundation 2006).

In a number of small steps, we have moved from Asperger Syndrome via social anxiety to alcoholism. It is very likely that Matt is not the only person with AS who has used alcohol as a coping strategy for tolerating the neuro-typical world.

The final word is from a young woman with Asperger Syndrome:

> Q: Is there a link between anxiety and drinking alcohol for you?
>
> A: Yes, because when I am drunk I don't care as much whether people secretly don't want to talk to me. Normally I am constantly aware of the possibility that I am not acting appropriately, and I stress out about it. Being drunk enables me to be someone else, superficially closer to the way that other people are.

Key Points

○ Alcohol is widely recognized as a means of managing the anxiety associated with social situations, and many individuals report that they drink in order to feel more confident socially.

○ Asperger Syndrome is characterized by a difficulty in social interaction and also by high levels of anxiety in many individuals. There are estimated to be significant numbers of individuals with Asperger Syndrome who also experience social anxiety disorder.

○ Several studies have indicated that those with social anxiety disorders have an above average chance of developing alcoholism.

CHAPTER 2

CHILDHOOD AND ADOLESCENCE - WHERE DOES IT START?

Childhood

For a child with Asperger Syndrome, the world is a very confusing and frightening place to be. These children often need consistent routines in order to feel safe and relaxed and may experience stress and anxiety from a very young age. Due to a tendency to use intellect rather than gut instinct, or intuition, to manage situations, they are working very hard to make sense of what is going on and hence can be in a constant state of awareness. This results in a greater chance of exhaustion, both physically and mentally (Attwood 2006). One of the most stress-producing environments is school, and some children may try to resolve this by avoiding it altogether. For those who do attend school, the home may be the only place of retreat, and after an exhausting day at school such children may wish to be alone in their room, do nothing but watch the TV, or engage in a range of release behaviours, which they have kept under control throughout the day. Some parents have commented that they find it hard to understand how their child can be fine all day yet be incapable of anything once at home. This may be because all of the capacity for interaction is depleted, and re-charging must take place in the safety of home.

Bullying is commonplace amongst children and adults with AS. Tony Attwood (2006) quotes a figure of around 90 per cent of those with Asperger Syndrome experiencing bullying throughout their lives: a shockingly high figure, which demonstrates the ease with which other people, even children, can easily spot the difference in communication and interaction of a peer with AS.

When I was very young, I was aware that I had a high level of anxiety, although I wouldn't have known how to articulate it at the time. I have always had the feeling that the world is a place of unexpected changes and potentially great danger. This was not a way of thinking that I learnt from listening to friends and family, it was just an observation that I made from looking at the world around me. When I was taken to school by my mother, I had a dread of morning assembly. I hated the idea of being arranged in rows and being part of a large group of pupils in the school hall. I can recall asking my mother the same question every day. 'Assembly won't last long, will it?' She would always reassure me that no, it wouldn't last long. For the first few months of my time at primary school, I would ask this question every day. My mother showed remarkable forbearance in never losing her temper despite the repetition of this question, in my opinion!

Every morning was a time of low-level anxiety and dread which I did my best to deal with on my own. When we moved house in 1968 (when I was seven), I not only had to adapt to a new environment, but also to a new school. I remember this time clearly. I remember my clumsiness (a trait I have to this day), and my being very good in my class at reading, but hopeless at any of the practical tasks that involved using scissors or making things from paper and glue. The persistent feeling of dread and anticipation which filled me was to become the constant emotional background noise of my childhood. I was very good at remembering facts and figures, but manipulating data in the cause of solving problems was a skill which has never come easily to me. I have been aware of this all my life, but have only relatively recently been able to express the feeling this gave me inside.

I might have received praise for knowing certain things and for being able to read very well, with a huge vocabulary, but I was aware that I had severe cognitive deficits when it came to being 'creative': that is, being original and being able to transform data into something new. I have always been hugely impressed by people who could do this quite easily. Whenever people said that I was intelligent, I was always aware that I didn't feel that this was the case. I was able to recall a lot of information, but intelligence for me was the ability to translate something into a new form, or solve problems. I have always felt as though I have a pair of mental handcuffs on my thought processes. I was able to comprehend what needed to be done, but was unable to actually follow through and do it myself.

Fascinations and interests

Part of the diagnostic criteria for AS involves narrow, absorbing interests which engulf the individual and become the focus of every waking thought. This is a trait which continues into adulthood, but is perhaps more noticeable in younger people with the condition, who have not yet learned that sometimes other things have to take priority over the study of lamp bulbs, or whatever the interest happens to be. The motivation behind the desire to gain extensive knowledge about a specific topic is perhaps to gain a sense of control in a world where much feels out of control. The pursuit of knowledge is very much an AS characteristic, and topics chosen tend to be fact based rather than idea based, with a preference for those where there are definite right and wrong answers, rather than lots of undecided possibilities. These interests can be passing and last a few days, weeks, or months, or they can stand the test of time and last a lifetime. There are suggestions that many academic professors may have significant characteristics of AS due to their long-term expertise and devotion to one area of research!

My special areas of fascination (that I now know to be part of the diagnosis of AS) during this period included Nelson's Column and, by extension, Nelson himself; the Battle of Britain; dinosaurs (but in a very fact-driven way, i.e. their height, weight, which era they lived in, and so on); Tutankhamun; and horror films, particularly the Universal Studios films of the thirties and forties, and the Hammer Studio films made at Bray between the fifties and seventies. In my teens, I used to travel to the West End of London on Saturdays and spend all day in the cinema section of Foyle's bookshop, at that time the biggest bookshop in the UK, as well as the Cinema Bookshop in Great Russell Street. I would spend hours trawling through books on the cinema of the macabre, as though on a never-ending quest to take in as much information about certain subjects as I could tolerate. It felt (and indeed still does) like a form of hunger for knowledge, one in which I actually felt intellectually famished and needed information as nutrition.

My interest in horror films became so great that I used to tape the soundtrack of my favourite films when they were broadcast on the TV, then transcribe the entire script into a notebook, supplementing it with credits derived from my extensive collection of books on the subject. I also recall keeping a diary of every film shown on television over the course of a year, including times, channels and dates of transmission. I did not attempt to watch all of these films, only to record their existence.

I used to collect all the cards which came free with Brooke Bond tea and kept all the books in which they were kept together.

My parents encouraged me in my interests, even to the extent that my father had a leather-bound blank book made, with 'Matthew Tinsley's History of Horatio Nelson' block printed on the cover in gold leaf! These interests became known as 'Matt's phases' and they were viewed with wry amusement, as they came with the knowledge that they would burn very brightly for a specific period of time and then be superseded by a different passion. As they didn't cause me to get into any trouble, I was left alone to get on with them.

Later in my teens, I became intensely interested in the rivalry between Steve Ovett and Sebastian Coe, festooning my bedroom with items cut from newspapers, and even managing to get Coe's autograph as the centrepiece of this display. I memorized all the times and dates of their record-breaking feats and was always hunting through newspapers and magazines for any articles about them

Adolescence

The teenage years are difficult for any young person, flooded with hormones, expectations and changing boundaries. Those with AS are hit harder than most; not only do they experience the same physiological effects as any other young person, they also have the added stress of dealing with friendships and changes, neither of which are easy for them. The move from primary to secondary school is a big one, with independence expected and organization of self required. Change is not high on the list of favourite things of any person with AS, yet adolescence brings plenty. From having one teacher and one classroom at primary school, secondary school typically brings multiple teachers, a far bigger building to find your way around and a new classroom for every lesson. The school may be three or four times larger than the previous one: and bearing in mind that people are the main issue for those with AS, this problem may be multiplied by 400 per cent at a new school. The confusion that the young person feels may be directed inwards as depression and withdrawal, or outwards as aggression and difficult behaviour. Matt found his own way to cope with his continuing feelings of panic and dread.

My general anxiety during all of this time was still incredibly high, again with no obviously explicable source for it. As I entered my teens, I discovered that the benzodiazepines (tranquillizers), which my mother had been prescribed, were wonderful as a short-term aid to my extreme nervousness. I became addicted to these and stole them without it becoming very easily noticed. My mother was suffering from severe depression and my father's time was spent caring for her when she was not at work, so it was simple for me to purloin a few to get me through particularly difficult times. Other methods for anxiety control involved sucking mints, which seemed to help psychologically, if not in any other way, as well as taking J Collis Browne's Mixture throughout my childhood, which tended to act as a calmative on my churning stomach and quelled my feelings of intense nausea and the desire to vomit. I have recently learned that this medication contains morphine, which may explain its numbing effect on my senses.

My time at secondary school was successfully navigated and improved considerably by joining Wandsworth School Choir, one of the most famous choirs in the country at the time. This entitled me to certain key privileges which eased my passage though life at a large, inner London comprehensive in the 1970s: an environment which could have been a nightmare for me to cope with. I was allowed to stay in the music rooms during break time, and lunchtimes were taken up with rehearsal, so I managed to pretty much evade the rough-and-tumble which would have been my lot out in the playground. I managed to spend most of my time within the 'safety' of the rehearsal rooms, and in the hall where we spent all our lunch hours practising for one of the many high-profile concerts that we did during my time there.

The history of the choir itself became another subject of intense fascination for me. I even visited the home of the choir master and was allowed to read all the press cuttings he kept on the subject. It was almost as though I needed to absorb as much information, however irrelevant it might have seemed to others, about any subject which interested me.

A combination of this lucky break, along with my, by now regular, use of the stolen medication, and being in one of the top streams of the school by ability, meant that my time there was much less stressful than might otherwise have been expected.

Activities and friends

Parents may be concerned that their child has few friends and little interest in activities. He or she may spend many hours playing computer games and interacting virtually, rather than with real people. This need to retreat may be very strong, and a balance may need to be established so as to encourage interaction without removing the very vital need for solitude and focus. The fascinations and interests that the person has, which may seem weird and obsessive to others, may play an important role in managing the world outside the bedroom door, and should not be banned or removed (unless they are harmful or illegal). It is preferable to set some boundaries around time and availability so that the person knows when the next opportunity to engage in the interest will be, whilst still being encouraged to fulfil his or her other obligations and broaden interests.

Friendships during adolescence change from those of earlier childhood, being less focused on play and more on interaction. This can also be a problem for adolescents with AS. Not good in groups (because each other person is a whole new set of confusing social behaviour to translate, multiplying the exhaustion and effort for the person with AS), they prefer to have one-to-one friendships. They may be excluded from group activities because they cannot cope or hide their differences well enough.

Outside of school, I had a couple of friends with whom I shared an interest in playing tennis, which became a common bond. Apart from these, I spent my adolescence pretty much in my room, listening to classical music. As I wasn't causing any trouble, and never gave my family much cause for complaint, I was left alone to get on with my solitude. Having sung in a performance of Mahler's Eighth Symphony at the Proms in 1975, I became obsessed with this piece of music, as did my father. He would spend most of his time listening to a piece of music, putting it on again and again, until we had ceased to even notice that it was being played. I listened to it every night for about a year or more (another intense fascination). I became lost in the music, and was blissfully unaware of the world outside, and of what I might be missing by not really participating in it. I was quite happy, and only in retrospect does it seem obvious to me that I was different from my peers at school, and that my lack of interest in close relationships or in anything social, apart from a couple of mates, was in any way out of the ordinary.

Alcohol in adolescence

A survey by the Youth Justice Board (2001), quoted on the government's Wired for Health website (Department of Health 2007), reports that between the ages of 11 and 16, over 80 per cent of young people will have tried alcohol. By the age of 13, drinkers outnumber those who don't drink (Balding 2000, quoted on the Wired for Health website). By the age of 15–16 years, 33 per cent of girls and 39 per cent of boys describe themselves as 'regular drinkers' (Mental Health Foundation 2006). Reasons cited by young people as to why they drink include:

- wanting to appear grown up and establish independence

- curiosity: testing the limits and experimenting

- conforming to others' expectations: modelling behaviour of peers and adults

- having a family experience of drinking.

Matt did not drink for any of these reasons. Conforming requires an ability to consider the world from another perspective, and to believe that that perspective (the views of others) matters more than your own, as well as a desire to be like everyone else. These are abilities that are less developed in someone with AS. Matt was late to start drinking regularly in comparison to other young people, but once he started and found this a successful means of managing his feelings of dread, he was unable and unwilling to stop. Drinking was not a social activity for him, and was a means by which he could experience the world as others around him were doing. In essence, alcohol made Matt 'normal'. He has spoken of being puzzled at this time as to why everyone else wasn't as drunk as he was. He had mistakenly assumed that others were experiencing the same levels of anxiety as he was and so would feel equal joy at finding a release from this. He was not aware that everyday life does not have such an extreme impact on those without AS, as they are able to integrate relatively easily with others, and translate the social and ever-changing world around them.

I was not at all interested in alcohol during my teenage years, although I did try it a couple of times with friends when no adults were around. I didn't really start drinking until I went to college at the age of 19 to study languages. I found student life to be a total mystery. I was studying in London, and remained at home with my parents whilst I studied. The idea of moving out and sharing a flat with other students did not occur to me at all. I was totally at ease at home. What on earth would I want to leave for?

I imagine that it was the stress of studying and of being in a classroom environment, which I had always found difficult to deal with, which led me to begin using alcohol as a tranquillizer to a greater extent. The fear of being 'put on the spot' by a lecturer, and of not understanding simple instructions in the class, was a source of great and constant tension to me. My sense of feeling stupid and of dreading the feeling of shame at being perceived as such hung over my days at college like a cloud. I would go out for drinks with my girlfriend, but never really socialized with other students at college. I would go straight home after studies, unless I was due to see my partner, and wasn't drinking too much whilst at home. However, as my studies progressed I found it was acceptable to drink at lunchtime (something which had never occurred to me before). I found that my studies in the afternoon were far more manageable, and I felt quite euphoric that I had found a method of making my lectures less distressing for myself. I felt secretly gleeful inside that I had found a legal way of dealing with hugely uncomfortable feelings of tension, which also did not make me stand out from the crowd. I would have a pint or two at lunchtime, and occasionally one after college on the way home, but rarely drank at home. The notion of buying my own alcohol to drink at home was one which didn't gain much currency with me until I started working after leaving college.

Key Points

- Characteristics of Asperger Syndrome are evident from early childhood and may include anxious or worrying behaviour.

- Teenage years are often the time when those with Asperger Syndrome become more aware of their social differences and experience increasing feelings of anxiety.

- Drinking alcohol to conform to peer expectations and enable social integration is typical teenage behaviour.

- A young person with AS may realize that alcohol can help to reduce feelings of anxiety and aid social interaction.

CHAPTER 3

THE ADULT SOCIAL WORLD - FRIENDSHIP, RELATIONSHIPS AND OTHER PEOPLE

Friendship

Those with AS are sometimes said to have an emotional maturity which is less developed than would be expected for their age, and I know that this is a characteristic that Matt readily identifies with, claiming he has got stuck mentally at around the age of 14. It is not uncommon for those with AS to find the company of their peers difficult, preferring to mix with those older or younger than themselves. This may be because there are different dynamics in such relationships than in peer age friendships. Older friends may be more tolerant of a younger person or appreciate the high level of knowledge that a person with AS may have on certain topics. They may be less concerned with being 'cool' and be more likely to take the person for who he or she is. A younger friend may look up to the person with AS and allow that person to be the dominant one in the relationship – possibly for the first time in his or her life. If you have experienced many years of bullying and exclusion from social activities, the opportunity to be the one looked up to is to be relished. Many people with Asperger Syndrome do want to have friendships and relationships, but struggle to understand the 'rules' and gain access to this world. The awareness of one's inability to do as one's peers are doing, along with the isolation which follows the many failed attempts, is a major cause of the depression and anxiety that affects so many with this condition. It is no wonder that some people turn to alcohol to try and facilitate the joining-in process. Many people with AS simply remain isolated and alone throughout their lives, unable to navigate the social arena. This also has knock-on effects throughout all areas of their lives. Research shows that children without friends may be at risk of developing mental health issues in adulthood (Hay, Payne and Chadwick, in Attwood 2006). Limited contact with others as a child may also impact on the individual's ability to establish relationships as an adult, as essential skills will not have been learned – conflict management, trust, sharing feelings, sharing possessions (Attwood 2006).

> I have no friends who I see automatically every day, week or month. I never go out in a group and never consider inviting a group to be with me. (Male with Asperger Syndrome)

> Frankly, I have no friends. I know some people. But there is no one I can honestly say I have a relationship with that could be described as a 'friend'... It's mostly about not knowing how to do it, and the pain of trying and failing far outweighs any benefit that I could possibly perceive coming from friendship. (Male with Asperger Syndrome)

> I generally spend my time alone in my room. A lot of my social interactions are conducted over the internet. (Female with Asperger Syndrome)

I had few friends as I was growing up, but those I had I was very close to. Most of the sharing that we did was in pursuits such as playing football, tennis, bowls and also going away on holidays with other members of their family. At secondary school the friends I made were generally those in the outstanding school choir that I joined at the beginning of my time there. My closest friends were generally younger than me, as I seemed to have more in common with these people. I rarely, if ever, went to parties. Most of the 'fun' that I had revolved around playing sport and other games, and listening to music and watching television.

Relationships

There has been some work and writing around AS and relationships (Aston 2003; Henault 2006; Hendrickx 2008; Hendrickx and Newton 2007; Stanford 2003). Many adults with AS do not have any relationships throughout their lives, but there are some who do, and sometimes these are successful. Matt has said that he doubts that he would have ever been married were it not for the alcohol that allowed him to be flexible and less rigid than his natural state.

For individuals who have had limited friendships through childhood and possibly been bullied and excluded on a regular basis, the idea of approaching a potential partner is very stressful. They may have very few social contacts with whom to go to a pub or other social event and so may not know how to go about meeting new people. The internet has helped many people with AS to make links with people through online forums, special interest group sites and dating sites.

> Internet dating is the ideal medium: it allows pre-selection filtering, and, because in the early stages it mostly involves anonymous forms of communication (email), the gaucheness (physical, spoken, appearance) isn't so pervasive to the eye (mind) of the recipient. This reduces the chances of being dismissed immediately. (Male with Asperger Syndrome)

Many of those who do attempt relationships find the demands and expectations placed upon them by their partner difficult to deal with. They may wish to continue going about their lives in the same way that they did when single, and become defensive when it is suggested to them that things have changed now that there is a partner to consider. The notion of empathy and compromise is very difficult for some with AS to comprehend due to a reported less developed ability to empathize and see another's perspective. A need for routine and predictability can be problematic, if, for example, the person needs to eat at a specific time or only eats certain foods, or cannot tolerate people dropping by unannounced. A partner brings a whole new existence to the person with AS and can add a whole load more stress and anxiety.

This stress can lead to drinking behaviour as the person attempts to cope with the requirements of the new partner and hide his or her own differences and habits, perhaps all too aware that they are unusual. This can be a big problem in a relationship!

But this doesn't have to be the case. If there is a good understanding of AS by both partners and an acceptance of each other's different way of seeing the world, then successful relationships are possible for those with AS.

During my teens, I did have a small circle of friends, most of whom are still friends to this day. I was not at all interested in looking for a girlfriend. Frankly, I would not have had the first clue what to do, where to look or how to behave, so I simply put any notion of a girlfriend to the back of my mind. None of the usual arenas for meeting girls (clubs, pubs, bars, etc.) appealed to me in the slightest at this point.

Attraction and selection of partners

There is some evidence (Hendrickx 2008) that the selection criteria of a potential partner are slightly different for those with Asperger Syndrome than for the general population. Amongst those questioned for research, one of the most popular responses was that the level of interest shown in the person with AS by the potential partner was a large part of initial attraction. This seemed to be for a number of reasons:

- Lack of self-esteem: those with AS do not feel they have the right to be interested in or pursue someone who has not shown interest in them.

- Fear of rejection or ridicule: declaring one's interest may lead to one being rejected or laughed at.

- Sense of logic: it seems pointless and a waste of time to spend time desiring someone who is not interested.

Other factors mentioned that are an important part of initial attraction are:

- intelligence
- shared interests

- specific physical features (often hair)
- an ability to act as a social interpreter
- good organizational skills
- motivation
- capability
- an absence of negative stress.

The type of person attracted to someone with AS is reported to be one of two types: a very empathic and nurturing person; or someone who has equally strong aspects of autism, or is eccentric or neuro-diverse in some other way (Grandin 2006).

- *The empathic partner:* takes on a caring, supportive role in the relationship, realizing that his or her partner finds life quite difficult – those with AS can appear vulnerable and child-like and are said to have symmetrical, angelic faces, which are appealing (Attwood 2006). Problems can occur if the empathic partner requires high levels of emotional or intuitive support, which the AS partner may have no concept of unless clearly directed. Empathic partners may feel that they are not loved due to limited verbal or physical displays of care by the AS partner. They may not understand that the AS partner may demonstrate love in different ways, which they do not recognize. This can lead to mutual frustration where both partners misunderstand the other's motives.

- *The eccentric or similarly AS partner:* such partners may have a natural understanding of the thought process of their fellow AS partner. They may have different emotional needs and a more logical brain, which appreciates the efforts made by the partner. There may be shared interests and solidarity in being equally socially excluded or awkward. This type of partnership is shown to be successful (Hendrickx 2008).

I met my first girlfriend whilst visiting a local girls' public school that had invited us to attend their sessions preparing pupils for the Oxbridge entrance examination. We had locked horns in some debates in the class, and I found her intellect hugely attractive. I have always maintained that it is the mind of a woman that attracts me – her appearance is of secondary consideration, although of course it is of some consideration! I adore women with whom I can have a meeting of minds on the intellectual level. Without that, none of the other facets of a relationship are relevant to me. We dated for a year, and our relationship ended when she went up to Oxford and started seeing someone there.

I was devastated. I felt that I had lost the only chance I would ever have to be in a relationship. I didn't understand that I was merely going through what most people have to endure in their lifetimes – relationships coming to their natural conclusion. I believed that this was my only chance of a relationship – a typical example of the black-and-white thinking that comes with AS, I suppose.

I was sick with loss for over six months, and only felt that I could get over what had happened about a year later. My next partner was a mature student, eight years older than me, whom I met at university. In what was to be the usual turn of events, I let the other person take the initiative in making the running in the relationship. This was to become a recognizable feature in my relationships, with my very passive nature in this regard coming to the fore. This was the relationship which got me through my university years, as it were. My partner was very nurturing and capable, was a good sounding board for my assorted anxieties, and didn't mind the nature of my various quirks. In fact, it was to become a pattern, I believe; my partners seemed to find the nature of my routines and interests appealing, perhaps invoking a feeling of 'motherliness' in them. I didn't realize this at the time, being totally unaware of the possibility of my having a 'condition' such as AS; it has only become more apparent to me in retrospect.

My then partner enabled me to get through such trials as a year spent abroad studying as part of my degree course. I lived in both France and Italy for this time, learning the languages. We studied together in the same universities for much of the time, and I was able to visit her when she lived in a different town nearby. I must admit, my experiences of mixing with the natives and learning French and Italian were probably not what my tutors would have expected. I spent much of the time in my room, or wandering around town looking in shop windows, rather than getting to know people and immersing myself in the language. I did spend quite some time reading foreign newspapers, as well as the English ones I spent hours hunting down to fill my need for information about home.

Upon our return to the UK we stayed together for a year, but broke up due to our constant bickering. This was probably due partly to my need to have as much time to myself as I required, without feeling beholden to anyone else that I should be available to fulfil their needs. This is a character trait that I am very aware is still strong in me, and one which I doubt will ever change.

Alcohol and relationships

There are a number of factors which may increase the likelihood of increased drinking in association with relationships. These are common to all relationships, but the more rigid nature and limited social understanding of someone with AS may mean that these factors cannot be tolerated to the same degree as by a non-AS person.

Relationship issues that may increase a person's tendency to drink:

- The need to compromise one's own routines: not being able to engage in relaxing activities.

- The need to compromise one's own favourite activities: less time doing specific interests.

- Having to engage in activities that the partner wants: doing something one doesn't want to do can be difficult and stressful for someone with AS.

- Trying to work out the needs of another person: not a natural AS skill.

- Having to consider the needs of another person (once you know what they are).

- Having to compromise the need for solitude and one's own space.

- Conflict and disagreements: criticism is very poorly received and tolerated by many with AS.

- Dealing with unexpected emotional reactions: how to respond in the 'right' way, as expected by the partner.

- Responding to demands and expectations: curtailments to individual freedom, rules, boundaries and permitted behaviour, as dictated by the partner.

- Having to share living space with another person and his or her possessions.

- Having responsibility for another person, and, potentially, children.

- Managing the relationship on top of other pressures, such as work (this can have a cumulative effect).

- Having to deal with the end of a relationship.

All through this time, my alcohol consumption was steady without being what I would have considered dangerous. I think my serious drinking began upon entering the world of work properly for the first time in 1984, when I was about 22 years of age. It was then that I started seeing the woman who became my first wife. We had met at university and become friends. When my previous relationship ended, we started going out. She was another woman with a great intellect, and a member of Mensa, and once again, I was probably attracted more to her mind than her body, although I did find her very attractive as well! She was hugely organized and disciplined, and got a job as a legal PA, which looking back was again ideal for me, as I had someone practical to 'look after' me, although I never consciously thought about the relationship in those terms. When we went on holiday, she was in charge of all the practical arrangements, and when we bought a flat together, she ran the household, more or less.

I was finding keeping a work life and a home life going very difficult. The stress of trying to be social at work, and sharing a small studio flat with very little space for one person, let alone two, meant that my drinking had increased markedly.

In addition, huge financial stresses due to high mortgage costs for the flat we had bought added to my general state of anxiety. I would buy a bottle of Famous Grouse whisky (the smell of which I cannot bear any more, associating it as I do with a time of great misery) and hide it in one of my bags. This would usually last me a day or two. Once my partner had left for work, I would pour a wine glass full of Scotch and add a couple of ice cubes. I would sup this while watching the television, before ensuring that I brushed my teeth, sprayed myself with aftershave and eaten plenty of mints, all to disguise the reek of alcohol on the way into work in the morning, as well as when I arrived there. Once at work, I would go out to collect coffees for everyone, and sneak half a pint of lager in the five minutes it took me to go to the local café. I would go for a couple of pints of strong lager at lunchtime, and then have some more after work in the pub on the way home, often with workmates. This would be the easiest way I knew to socialize. I would also wander the streets of the West End with a small bottle of whisky or brandy in my pocket, and steal swigs from it when I perceived that no one was watching.

I found this period of my life so stressful, that for many years afterwards I avoided using the District Line on the London Underground to Wimbledon when I visited my family. I associated it so strongly with anxiety, unhappiness and depression that I would take a more convoluted route involving mainline trains and buses, even though it would take me much longer. Even now, almost 20 years later, I still get a pang of anxiety when I take this particular tube line.

Eventually, having separated once and then getting married, we split up for good, as we did not seem to be able to find a connection in our relationship, and had begun living what could be considered as separate lives. I didn't care too much at the time, as long as I could blunt any sensation of loss or despair by getting drunk, and medicating myself with strong cider or whisky.

I moved out and, after staying with a friend for a month, eventually ended up renting a room in the house of a lawyer who was often not at home due to his work. It was here that I managed for a while to cut down on my alcohol, and also started dating the woman who would become my second wife, and who I had met at work. Having made the decision to leave a relationship which was working for neither me nor my wife, I felt a profound sense of relief. In addition, not sharing my bedroom was a pleasure that I hadn't experienced for a long time. The sense of separateness and self which I recognize now as being hugely important for me gave me an enormous sense of relief. I was no longer answerable to anyone for their happiness, as I had felt to be, rightly or wrongly, whilst married. The lawyer with whom I shared the flat became a very good friend. I relied upon him to help me solve problems and give me a sense of perspective whenever life seemed to overwhelm me. I actually felt that I was beginning to get a grip on my alcohol intake. I would still drink a lot of beer, but my consumption of spirits dropped considerably. I even felt confident enough to tell my new partner that I had a drink problem, in order to give her the option of not proceeding with our relationship. In fact, this wasn't to lead to the end of our relationship for another ten years.

As usual, I had followed my usual practice of slowly getting to know someone, to measure her up, almost circling her and learning to know her very well before I would consider going out with her. I have always done this. I have never been interested in casual dating or short-term relationships, as I would much rather be doing my own thing rather than make compromises in a relationship which has no long-term future. I need to know that the relationship is going to last, or at least has the potential to be long-term, before I will countenance going out with someone. I tend to make that person the centre of my universe. In fact, since my diagnosis I have often been asked how I cope with relationships with my condition. I reply that I find that my partner becomes a 'special interest or fascination' in a category of her own, and I learn as much as I can about her, her fears, foibles, tastes and ways. I will remember casual comments made by my partner months previously about a particular like or desire, and I will ensure that I attempt to accommodate in furnishing whatever it is, to the best of my ability.

My wife was in charge of running the household, as I have mentioned previously. She organized all the bills into folders, made sure the payments were made on time, and generally ensured the smooth running of the house. My total lack of practicality would have been a recipe for disaster, if it had been left to me to do such tasks, although I think I may now be able to cope with a certain level of responsibility. My problem is in not being able to foresee situations that may arise which require forward planning. This could have led to disaster.

One of the main problems in all my relationships was that I didn't take my partners' concerns seriously. Any problems with our relationship or my drinking were brushed under the carpet in my mind. Alcohol meant that I never felt the full level of shame or discomfort when challenged about my drinking, and I used to drink more just to cover up feelings of guilt and inadequacy. My partners may have been seething, but I never really internalized their unhappiness. I suppose this was part of the lack of theory of mind; if *I* felt fine about things, even if this sensation was alcohol induced, then how could *they* have a problem? Looking back, this makes a lot of sense to me. The notion that they had their own unhappiness or problems simply didn't register with me, if I perceived no difficulties myself.

My problem with anger was that it was so intense inside that I daren't let it out. I would prefer to switch off emotionally. I was once asked about my anger when I was in rehab. I told the counsellors something I had never revealed before. I felt that if I was to let all my anger out without containing it in any way, I would end up smashing myself to pieces around the room. I would attack the walls and break as many bones as I could in a fit of rage. I have often punched the wall several times when my partners were there, in an attempt to expend anger on inanimate objects. The ultimate step I have always felt I would take if I lost control would be to cut my face up with a very sharp knife, disfiguring myself in my rage. I have always felt this, but the only time I ever told anyone was at rehab. I have never been pushed this far, but I have always kept it as an option, to be used only when I have lost all control.

I suppose my partners knew that there was very little chance of me giving up alcohol, so they decided to stay whilst it was still worth being in the relationship. My second wife did give me an ultimatum, her or the drink, and I couldn't give her an answer, which just about says it all. I couldn't see a life without either of them, although now I have exactly that!

Solitude and space

Another issue for people with AS is their need for regular and perhaps extended periods of solitude in order to cope with life and the needs of a partner. This can feel very rejecting and hurtful to the partner, who may not understand that it is not a personal affront, but a need to escape all of mankind. The world can be exhausting for a person with AS, who has to work hard at making sense of the confusing non-verbal signals and 'rules' of the social world. Thus, he or she may suffer 'overload' from the demands of life – both in terms of sensory perception and mental effort. It is important that people with AS have some 'switching off' time. Failure to have sufficient time out can lead to anger, depression and increased alcohol or substance consumption. However, the AS partner may not realize that his or her withdrawal can equate to rejection, abandonment and punishment to the non-AS partner (Hendrickx 2008). Thus, it requires mutual learning to appreciate each other's perspective and needs.

> Sometimes I feel myself distancing even with my partner, whom I love dearly. It's almost like my emotions need a rest. (Male with Asperger Syndrome)

> [When alone] I do very little both physically and mentally. This time is not spent pondering or thinking: my head is empty. I am

devoid of thoughts, and therefore, stress. It is like a shutdown of all extraneous processes. This downtime is vital for me to be able to cope with the rest of life around other people. (Male with Asperger Syndrome)

I began a new relationship at the age of 32, once separated from my wife. Once again, this was someone who had made her interest in me clear, so I didn't need to worry that I might face rejection. Also, she was a very nurturing person, with whom I found it extremely easy to communicate. I found that my new girlfriend was intelligent and quite gentle, with the ability to be self-deprecating and laugh at the absurdities of life. I find that the world around me seems absurd most of the time, so to find someone to share this world view was especially pleasing. We ended up moving in together at my instigation. Interestingly enough, I made the decision when extremely drunk – almost as though it gave me 'permission' to do something which I knew I 'ought' to do but that I wasn't sure about. It seemed to be the logical next step in our relationship, one that would seem perfectly natural. However, I had been unsure about sharing a home with someone again, and had considered that a relation-ship might work much better if the couple lived apart. This would enable them to have their own space and to have time when they could pursue their own interests. However, having been with my partner for over two years, and having been on holiday abroad with her, I felt secure enough in my knowledge of her to take the risk of trying to share a home. I had also found that having consumed alcohol my mind felt 'freer' to take risks and make leaps of logic that never came naturally when I was sober. It is almost as though the straight lines and logical thinking, the 'cage' of imagination which was my normal default position, were removed by my drinking, liberating me to be a totally different person to my normal sober self. I didn't feel so concerned about possible consequences of my actions once I was 'loosened' up by alcohol.

I found that living with my new partner was relatively straightforward, perhaps because my alcohol intake increased to deal with the change in my circumstances. I now had to take another person's wishes into account. I was beginning to attempt to hide my drinking (as much as that was possible) by drinking outside the home, and also concealing the supplies of spirits that I was bringing into the flat. If my partner went to the lavatory or went downstairs to put some rubbish out, this was a cue for me to get some of my hidden stash of drink and to swig as much as possible in the short time available. This was always accompanied by a burst of guilt and worthlessness. I was very aware that this was an unsustainable way of living, built on both addiction and deception. There was a gradual increase in my intake. Unconsciously, I realize now, I was finding sharing a home to be a difficult way of life to maintain without the deadening effects of drink. Not being able to please myself whenever I liked, and being aware of the necessity of sharing, which did not come naturally to me, were things to be endured, helped by the anaesthetic effect of booze.

I would still need my own space and time, especially at Sunday lunchtimes, when I would go to my usual pub and read my usual paper in exactly the same order every week. I would sit in a corner and try to lock out my surroundings while I concentrated on world events, which I have always found fascinating. I guess that this is because I am striving to understand the mechanics of the world, the politics, and the way everything works. If you have the raw material, in the form of news items, then it may be possible to gain a clearer picture of how everything in the world is organized. That is one of the reasons that I read all the British broadsheet papers online every morning when I wake up. I did this even when we had guests due for lunch, as there was simply no way I felt able to change my routine. The rest of the day would feel 'wrong' and irretrievably spoilt if I didn't manage to adhere to this familiar pattern.

In the evenings I would often leave my partner alone in the living room watching TV while I found my own space in the bedroom. There I could read what I wanted or watch another programme on TV. It also gave me the opportunity to have another secret drink from the supplies I had previously hidden in one of the various caches in the bedroom. This preference for spending time alone was not based on any dislike or negative feelings for my partner; rather, once again, a need for separateness and my own space, time to unwind from the day and just be at peace with myself. I have always found that what is going on in my head requires my undivided attention, whilst I go through my thoughts without any distraction, even from people I care about very much.

Socializing

For many people, alcohol and socializing go hand in hand. In our society we look at people who do not drink with suspicion, as if they are in some way spoiling the party for everyone else. Or perhaps there is a secret envy that these people do not need alcohol to lubricate the mind and release the stress. Either way, drinking is a very common pastime for the majority of adults. A recent survey reported that 73 per cent of men and 60 per cent of women had had a drink in the previous week (Mental Health Foundation 2006).

Of the people questioned, those with AS who did not drink seemed to be unconcerned by these social pressures; this tendency to follow one's own path, although not always of benefit socially, can help avoid peer pressure and potentially harmful behaviours.

> When I didn't drink at all it seemed to upset people. (Male with Asperger Syndrome)

> It is costly both in monetary terms, and physical and mental health terms. It simply makes no sense at all. I enjoy a cup of tea more than a glass of wine, so I drink tea. (Male with Asperger Syndrome)

> My sobriety is what sets me apart from people who could be my friends. I have reluctantly been to a bar, and a club, and a party. In each event, all I could see was a horde of drunken idiot assholes wasting time and money. (Male with Asperger Syndrome)

There are a number of studies on the general population that focus on the use of alcohol for self-medication of anxiety and other mental health issues. It is suggested that many of these individuals do not have a diagnosis of a mental health condition, and are therefore not receiving any other support (medication, counselling, etc.). These same people may also be unlikely to have a diagnosis of AS. This is particularly so if they are older, as there has only been an awareness of Asperger Syndrome in the English language since the late 1980s, with the original work only being translated from German in 1991.

One such study, as quoted in the Mental Health Foundation's *Cheers?* report on the relationship between alcohol and mental health states that, 'people with high social anxiety who use alcohol repeatedly to relieve their stress may come to rely upon it as their primary coping strategy, and research suggests that such people are at risk for alcoholism' (Mental Health Foundation 2006, p.19). The same study found that nearly half the people questioned reported that alcohol made them feel less inhibited and more confident, with around 50 per cent of this sample drinking above the recommended limits. Over 40 per cent said they drank alcohol in order to 'fit in'.

For those with AS who were asked, drinking alcohol did play a part in helping some of them socialize:

> I often drink on my own before going out, so that I am confident when I arrive rather than being anxious at first. Then I drink more while I am out. (Female with Asperger Syndrome)

> Alcohol gave me something in common with other people – it helped me function socially. (Male with Asperger Syndrome)

> I am less afraid of novel things when drunk, which is why I am quite happy to talk to strangers and go to new places without having someone familiar with me. (Female with Asperger Syndrome)

> I agree in part [that drinking is a social activity], but it's also a solitary activity conducted amongst groups of people that I do not belong to, as a means of forgetting that I am not one of them. (Female with Asperger Syndrome)

Social interaction is one of the key differences for those with AS. The difficulty in reading facial expressions, making eye contact and understanding the unspoken rules of social relationships makes any type of social event potentially stressful. While the work or school environment has a certain element of structure and clearly defined rules, the adult world of the pub, café or restaurant has little or no structure, and no clearly defined 'role' for the person with AS to play. Subjects of conversation change rapidly, and some with AS find their mental processing to be somewhat slower in taking in all of the details than their non-AS counterparts. Some people have said that they only feel confident in talking about subjects that they know a lot about, and so will remain totally silent when the conversation moves away from these topics, unable to improvise, lie or change the subject with the finesse required to do so. Overall, they can appear gauche, awkward, up-tight and unable to take a joke, often taking what is intended as harmless 'banter' as an insult. It is no wonder that many people with AS simply give up and retreat into a solitary world. Those that remain in this stressful arena may well turn to alcohol to provide a layer of 'padding' and numbness to protect them from the harsh confusion of the social world.

My work life would sometimes involve joining other people for a drink after work. Here I was well known for taking my newspaper out and starting to read it when I was in company. This had never struck me as wrong or particularly odd. I wanted to do it, therefore I did it. What could be the matter with that? However, I was treated to some joshing from my work colleagues, who would accuse me of rudeness. I would stop eventually, but with an internal shrug, and no sense of guilt or shame that I was being antisocial. I was simply being true to myself, and I wouldn't have minded if others did the same.

Any social life I had always revolved around being able to drink. The notion of meeting someone for a coffee, like I do now, would have struck me as ridiculous. What was the point of meeting someone if I had no alcohol? Why would I bother? How would I cope with the chit-chat and the social part of the meeting if I had no booze to relax me or to make my mind function in a way that was acceptable, in my own eyes anyway?

I would become intensely irritable and yearn to get away from a meeting where I had no access to alcohol. Part of this may have been because I was physically craving it, but also partly because I didn't know how to interact whilst sober.

Key Points

○ Using alcohol as a social lubricant is common practice for many people.

○ For those with AS, alcohol may be used to enable a tolerance and flexibility within friendships and relationships that may otherwise not have been possible.

○ Those with AS who drank alcohol gained access to social relationships and networks.

○ Those with AS who did not drink tended to avoid social situations and had fewer social contacts and relationships.

○ There are many factors within a personal relationship that may cause anxiety for a person with AS, which may lead to increased alcohol consumption.

CHAPTER 4

EMPLOYMENT – DRINKING AND THE WORKPLACE

Asperger Syndrome and the workplace

As a group, those with AS are typically hugely under-employed. A survey by the National Autistic Society (Barnard *et al.* 2001) found that only 12 per cent of adults with Asperger Syndrome, who by definition do not have a learning disability, were in full-time employment. This compares with 49 per cent of the disabled population as whole, which includes those with learning and physical disabilities. It is a shockingly low figure for a group whose main impairment is in interacting with the world. Amongst the users of Aspire, a UK-based mentoring project for adults with Asperger Syndrome, around 40 per cent of users had degrees or higher qualifications and yet less than 10 per cent were employed in any way at all. All of those that did work had part-time jobs that did not represent their qualifications, typically working in retail, care homes or admin jobs. Interestingly, perhaps, none of these people drank alcohol!

The type of difficulty that people with AS experience in the workplace is not necessarily connected to their ability to perform the tasks required, although without adequate instruction this could cause stress and problems.

Some potential issues that may arise for someone with AS through the entire process of job seeking are as follows:

Selecting and applying for work

- A possibly unrealistic assessment of own abilities: a tendency to either over- or under-estimate strengths and areas for development.

- A lack of motivation to work: the person may feel unable to manage work, or have little interest in 'climbing the ladder'.

- Difficulty planning or meeting application deadlines.

- Literacy difficulties: some people struggle to articulate themselves despite high academic capability.

- A dislike of interaction, for example, telephoning for more information regarding the job.

- An inability to 'lie', 'blag' or present self in the best light on the application form.

- A dilemma over whether or not to disclose AS: the person may not have an official diagnosis, or may fear discrimination.

- If the person chooses to disclose, the employer may not know what AS is or how it impacts on performance.

- If the person chooses not to disclose, there may be problems later.

Interview

- AS can be an invisible condition, and sometimes the lack of presentation of characteristics may mask difficulties. Equally, the presentation of AS may mask skills and abilities.

- Punctuality: the person may struggle with the concept of timing in order to arrive on time.

- An inability to imagine suggested scenarios: those with AS can find abstract thought and hypothetical questions and concepts difficult to answer or imagine.

- Difficulty answering open questions, e.g. 'Can you tell me how you feel about dealing with difficult people?' The person may not know what or how much information is required, or be able to relate the question to the context of the job.

- The difference in eye contact and non-verbal skills can give a misleading impression of motivation. Those who give little eye contact are seen as rude, deceitful, uninterested or disrespectful (personal communication 2007).

- The person may be unable to 'lie' or emphasize skills appropriate for the position.

- The environment may be a barrier to concentration and relaxation due to noise, lighting, distracting pictures or textures.

- The person may be anxious about not knowing what to expect, how many people will be in the room, how long the interview will last and what will be expected of him or her.

In the workplace

The person may have difficulty with:

- team working, and being required to see and take into consideration another's perspective

- accepting authority decisions regardless of own view

- social understanding: 'banter', pleasantries, reciprocity, making tea for everyone in the office, etc. in order to be part of the group

- environmental factors: there may be sensitivity to temperature, noise, light, etc.

- managing changes to structure, tasks, personnel and physical environment

- oral instructions: may struggle to understand full extent of what is said

- incomplete or brief instructions where 'gaps' are to be filled by the person

- decision-making, due to an inability to see the consequences of unknown courses of action

- eating or drinking with others, and may have specific dietary habits

- poor social skills: may appear rude or arrogant, and may be the victim or perpetrator of bullying

- verbal expression

- accepting feedback, as this tends to be perceived as criticism

- being assertive.

We will look at strategies to better support those with AS in the workplace in Chapter 7.

Alcohol and the workplace

The true extent of the scale of drinking in the work environment is difficult to measure accurately, as many people are able to successfully hide their drinking – as Matt did – for many years. Admitting to an employer that one has a problem with alcohol is extremely difficult: admitting the problem to oneself is hard enough for some people. Studies in the US suggest that problems caused by alcohol affect between 15 and 35 per cent of the working population (Alcohol Concern 2006a), and that 70 per cent of those with alcohol problems are in employment.

The problem may not be caused by actually drinking at work but by drinking during breaks or before a shift, or drinking to excess in the person's own time, such that he or she suffers from hangovers. These can all impair performance and be potentially dangerous both to the individual and to others around him or her (if the person operates machinery, for example). Such people may take more time off work with illness and be less efficient in their jobs. Around 15 per cent of all sick days are estimated to be alcohol-related, and it is cited that in 10 per cent of workplace accidents alcohol is a contributory factor. Alcohol Concern comments that 'Anxiety and depression are common psychiatric conditions that can predispose people to problem drinking to cope with personal and work-related problems' (Alcohol Concern 2006a, p.ii).

Work-related stress is named as a cause for drinking above safe limits. Common causes of stress at work include: ambiguity, overload, change, lack of clarity and lack of security (Alcohol Concern 2006a) – all issues that would be particularly difficult for a person with AS to cope with.

> I lost a job because of it [alcohol] and I lost my driving licence twice. (Male with Asperger Syndrome)

> It threw my working life in tatters. I think I took my education as far as I wanted to – it was the AS that affected that. As an alcoholic I went back to college and took my HNC and drank my way through it. (Male with Asperger Syndrome)

The death rates of individuals by profession is headed by those who work in pubs and bars, followed by doctors, seafarers and lawyers. These occupations are affected either by easy access to alcohol, stress, or long periods of boredom and being away from home. Writers are the next down the list!

One respondent, in education rather than employment, reported her experience of drinking through lectures:

> Sometimes I would go to lessons drunk, and I don't think it helped my concentration... Sometimes I drink so much that I feel too ill to go to university the next day. (Female with Asperger Syndrome)

Drinking after work is an accepted norm for many people who use it as a relaxant. For Matt, it was simply part of his overall strategy for getting through the day – work or no work.

> I learnt that drinking alcohol was an enabling factor for me from the outset of my working life. After graduating, I got a part-time job (through a friend, which was how I found most of my early work) working in the bookshop at a major theatre in London. When I graduated in 1984, I had no idea what to do next. Looking back, the lack of imagination that is a feature of Asperger Syndrome and related conditions is quite obvious to me. I had no strong inclination in a particular direction, and was drifting aimlessly, applying for jobs that I saw in the papers

occasionally, but never really following through. Perhaps I felt that I was just doing enough to stop being bothered by friends and family about my future, and I could point to the half-hearted efforts that I had already made as proof of my diligence. I spent much of my time reading about current affairs in the papers, a habit I have to this day. I can't understand why anyone wouldn't want to know what is going on in the world. I am beginning to understand that not everyone shares my point of view, but this revelation has been a long time coming.

The job at the theatre was quite low key, involving work in the stock room and covering breaks for the staff who were serving the public in the theatre foyers. It was a perfect first job after university. I loved the atmosphere of culture inside the theatre, but being in the stockroom most of the time meant that contact with the public was limited during the day to covering breaks for others. Attention to detail in the stockroom was another facet of the job which appealed to me: ensuring that the stock levels of different titles were correct, and that everything was in the right place for easy retrieval. There was a definite drinking culture here, and my friend and I would drink while we were working and put the pint glasses behind piles of books in the stockroom. When the stockroom was cleaned, we returned to the theatre bar around 40 pint glasses, which we had hidden to save us having to take them back on a daily basis. All this was seen as relatively normal, and I never had the cues that this behaviour was at all frowned upon. I felt quite comfortable working in this environment. The work was quite straightforward, the money was abysmal and the expectations were low. As long as I was paying attention to what I had to do, the work got done.

My next job was again found through a friend who was leaving the position I was to fill. This was a more stressful job, working in a small private modern art gallery in the West End of London. The gallery had a renowned mail order service, along with a small bookshop which was literally a 'shop window' for those who might want to order from us by mail or phone. My job was originally to deal with the packing and despatch of orders. However, when the manager left after three years, I was promoted to run the shop. This should have been a great achievement for me, but I immediately felt under pressure. I had to provide detailed weekly breakdowns of the shop's performance for the gallery owner. Cash flow was extremely tight, and part of the job was dealing with irate calls from suppliers demanding to be paid.

At the same time, there was a lot of alcohol available around the gallery, and the openings of shows were always awash with the stuff. As my financial problems increased at home, due to high mortgage rates, I began to drink more heavily and to a dangerous degree. In 1989 and 1990, around the age of 28, I was drinking a bottle of Scotch every two days, as well as super-strong beer and pints in the pub. A couple of wine glasses of Scotch was usually my breakfast, and I would also have some whenever I had the opportunity in the evening (usually while my girlfriend was in the bathroom). I would drink the strong beer as my 'official' drink in the evening, that being all that my partner was supposed to be aware of. At this point, I had severe internal pain, as my liver was damaged, but this didn't prevent me from drinking at all. I sensed that what I was undergoing was cirrhosis, but this knowledge couldn't counteract the overwhelming urge to consume more and more drink. I was under intolerable strain at home, finding it incredibly hard to make the mortgage payments, interest rates having gone up to 14 per cent. At the same time, I was spending much of my income on alcohol.

I see it as fortunate from a personal point of view that the gallery closed in 1992 due to the recession, and I was out of work for three months. I believe that my drinking would have reached an even more dangerous level if the gallery had remained open, and the financial plight had led to heavier demands on me. Even so, I spent most of this time drinking at home, and reading about world affairs in the newspapers. I applied for a job at a specialist foreign language bookseller at the suggestion of my wife; again, I hadn't sought the job myself, but let it be suggested to me, another example of my passive nature.

Fortunately, there was a position going free at the shop, and I started there in September 1992. I began again at the bottom rung, on the shop floor, but was quite happy that I had no responsibility for the financial side of the shop, or for dealing with angry suppliers or bosses.

Although I was given more responsibility as I stayed at the shop, I felt totally in control and happy with this. My first marriage had broken down and I had realized that the relationship had increased my stress level and drinking. I had begun a new relationship with my future second wife and my drinking had reduced. I was still drinking quite heavily, but this was more as a way of avoiding the unpleasantness of bad withdrawal symptoms than for any other reason.

I managed to manipulate my lunch breaks so that I would have time to myself – I never went when the majority of the rest of the staff did. I hated to sit in a small room in close proximity to everyone else, and to have to eat my lunch in front of them would have been even worse for me. I have never been good at sitting down with others and eating with them. I dislike the lack of privacy when I eat, and I prefer to be solitary and have some time to myself, rather than treat mealtimes as a social occasion.

I was also able to split my lunch breaks into two or three parts, and use the shorter breaks to slip to the pub to have a half pint of lager. This was generally to enable me to cope with the withdrawal symptoms of intense anxiety, shivering and hand tremors, nausea and a heart that seemed to race in time with my mind.

I have subsequently talked to a couple of people with whom I worked, and they say that I never appeared to be very drunk when at work, even though I might have consumed a couple of glasses of bourbon as my breakfast, a pint or two for lunch, and even have had a bottle of spirits secreted in my bag in the staff room. There may have been a smell of alcohol, it appears, but my behaviour at work was relatively unremarkable. As for myself, I just wanted to feel 'normal', and this was enabled by drink.

I maintained a reasonable work life for the next six or so years until I decided to leave and try a new job, again upon the invitation of a friend. This was to involve ordering and exporting technical manuals to various academic institutions throughout the Middle East. One of the clinching factors for this job (believe it or not) was that I could see Stamford Bridge, Chelsea FC's ground, from the office window: not the most reasoned-out or logical reason for accepting a job. The money was substantially more than I had been earning, and I also had the feeling that this was a job I 'ought' to take, in order to get on in life. I was aware that I was in a comfort zone at the foreign language bookshop, and wanted to prove to myself that I could succeed in a different workplace with a more demanding position. In addition, I had remarried the previous year, and my wife and I were thinking of starting a family. I believed that I had to get a better job in order to be a responsible husband and father. I took my cue for this from other people's experiences, my family and friends. I understood that when people married and had children, they worked hard and tried to progress for the sake of the family. I had no particular desire to do this, but I believed that in order to be seen as a success by other people, this was what was required.

The new job turned out to be a disaster for me on every level I can think of. I turned up for the job, and was more or less left to get on with learning the ropes with no formal training from the boss (my friend). I had no knowledge of Excel, which was a key part of the job, and some of the basics of Microsoft Office were learnt as I went along. I always need explicit instructions when learning a new skill, and find it almost impossible to be left alone and learn the skill without constant support and backup. Once I have mastered the skill, I am usually one of the best people at it, and find myself getting frustrated with others who are slower! I never seem to be able to remember the time when I myself found such a task difficult.

I had to deal with the shipping agents at Heathrow by regularly phoning them, and changing the instructions as to how the books were to be sent. There were continually changing instructions from my boss, and from his boss in the Middle East (the company's HQ). There was a constant edge of tension and urgency, and I felt that I was always teetering on the edge of disaster. My drinking escalated and I frequently drank at work. My incomprehension, and the constant feeling that I had stepped off a shallow ledge by a beach into very deep water, were never to leave me all the time I was there.

I realize now that I had picked just about the worst possible job for someone with ASC. The combination provided what I would describe as 'the Perfect Storm' for anyone with Asperger Syndrome, especially if this is undiagnosed and the person isn't even aware of the condition. I felt constantly stupid and useless inside, literally burning with the shame of my perceived inadequacy, going red with hot flushes. I dreaded the job so much that I started feeling nauseous by Saturday lunchtime at the thought of going to work on Monday morning. For me, the weekend lasted a mere 12 hours or so, which I attempted to extend through the consumption of more and more alcohol.

This job was where I became most aware of the discrepancy between my verbal abilities (allied to my memory), which had made me an ideal candidate for the positions I had previously held, and my information processing capabilities. Now I needed practical skills in computer programmes, and problem-solving skills in dealing with the various shipments of books, as well as an ability to cope with tighter deadlines than I had ever experienced before in the different places I had worked.

I was also expected to work extra hours, which I had not expected and was the last thing I desired: I just wanted to escape at the end of the working day, and to numb my unhappiness with drink. I was made redundant from this position and spent the next six months looking for work, but also drinking more heavily. I was not under any particular pressure at this point, but was addicted to alcohol as I can now openly acknowledge. I spent most of the summer in the local park, drinking super-strong beer and reading newspapers. I was applying for jobs throughout this time, without success, which didn't really bother me. Being in the park and drinking with no stress was for me a perfect existence at the time. I would look for vacant positions or send CVs to various bookshops in the morning, and spend the afternoon drinking. I didn't see any harm in this behaviour, as I *was* looking for work and also signing on. It was simply that I was also feeding my addiction whilst doing so. As I was doing all I could to find work (or so it felt to me at the time), my wife was not overly concerned, although money was very tight.

I was interviewed for another job in a specialist bookshop and was pleased to be offered the position. This was again a quite stress-free job, but I was becoming even more addicted to the drink. I was aware that a dark depression, which I had always felt lurking in the back of my mind, was now beginning to overwhelm me, which it finally did after six months. I could no longer function in the shop and was again made redundant. My drinking had been noted, and I was told that I couldn't be allowed in the shop with alcohol in my system.

Although I felt a certain amount of shame at this, I also felt relief. I knew that it was becoming impossible for me both to do my job properly and drink the amount of alcohol I needed to keep my, by now, severe withdrawal symptoms at bay. I suppose I knew that I ought to seek help, but I couldn't begin to guess how to go about this. I felt worthless and not deserving of assistance, which is a common sentiment amongst alcoholics, as I have since discovered. For the first time, my wife really lost her temper at my being unemployed again. She was, quite naturally, concerned about how we were going to manage without my salary, and she had also lost patience with me behaving in this way, drinking with no thought as to the consequences to other people. This was an impossible situation, as any attempt to work without drinking would have led to potentially lethal withdrawal symptoms, such as fits. As a result, this finally gave me permission to let myself admit that my depression, kept at bay by the need to work, was too much to deal with on my own. My wife accompanied me to see my GP, who diagnosed major clinical depression. However, knowing what the problem was did not improve our relationship at all, and relations between us at home became worse and worse. We were not communicating at all, and I would stay in the living room at bed time, just so that

I could avoid talking to my wife. I felt a sense of anger at the world, although I cannot really explain or understand the reasons behind this. This was to lead to the breakdown of my marriage, my separation and divorce.

I know that I would not have been able to keep the jobs that I have had in my life if I had not used alcohol to give me the tools to do so. Most people would say that drinking alcohol while working is unequivocally a bad thing, and that being sober makes you a much more effective employee. In my case, however, I firmly believe that I was only able to do the jobs, and also to put on the act of normality through sublimating my real self, because of alcohol.

Key Points

- The work environment is often very stressful for those with AS, particularly in relation to communicating with people, understanding what is required and managing the sensory stresses of the physical environment.
- Alcohol may enable tolerance of the working environment for some individuals with AS.

CHAPTER 5

BEGINNING OF THE END - A FAILING STRATEGY

Whilst drinking alcohol in moderation is relatively harmless to most people, there is a point where drinking is no longer a 'choice', but a 'need'. This may be the result of many years of heavy drinking, which has taken its toll on the body and created an addiction both to the chemicals ingested and to the effects.

There are many warning signs which may indicate an increasing reliance on alcohol and individuals will show and experience these differently. Some may successfully hide these for many years from close friends and family and it may not be until their body can cope no longer that the size of the issues becomes apparent. Typical signs of someone who relies on alcohol to get through the day may include:

- Planning activities to ensure that alcohol is always readily available.

- Short temper and irritability if alcohol is not available.

- Drinking alcohol before going out to social occasions – using it as more than a casual relaxant and social lubricant.

- Increasing and excessive consumption of alcohol.

- Genuine physical difficulty in coping without alcohol for any length of time – experiences nausea, sweats and shakes.

- Responsibilities and activities being forgotten or neglected as a result of drinking alcohol.

- Financial difficulties – debts arise as a result of spending large amounts of money on alcohol.

- Drinking in secret, hiding alcohol and financial details to conceal the extent of the drinking.

- Continuing to drink alcohol even after it has caused significant problems at work, home and in health.

For someone like Matt, the initial desire to manage his anxiety through drinking had become an addiction, not only as a coping strategy but also as a physical need to stave off the symptoms of alcohol withdrawal. It is a painful irony that even when trying to stop, a person is rewarded with highly unpleasant physical symptoms, which may include:

- hallucinations

- insomnia

- shaking and trembling

- convulsions and fitting

- blackouts

- increased heart rate

- anxiety and depression

- excessive perspiration

- nightmares

- vomiting and dry retching.

Health effects and other consequences

There are many health consequences to excessive and long-term consumption of alcohol. These range from the temporary and relatively harmless, such as a hangover, to life-threatening conditions, such as liver cancer. It is important for the individual to be aware of the very real risks of these effects and the consequences of continuing to consume alcohol.

One 29-year-old man, who had only just discovered that he had Asperger Syndrome, had developed epilepsy and hepatitis in the past year, having never experienced a fit previously. This was potentially as a result of excessive alcohol consumption, which he used to numb the constant panic attacks and anxiety that he felt.

> Drinking has given me short-term problems, such as feeling sick and having hangovers. I also tend to injure myself whilst drunk because I think it is a good idea to climb over fences rather than use gates, etc. (Female with Asperger Syndrome)

> I was told in my 30s that my liver function was that of a 70-year-old. I also have/had gout. (Male with Asperger Syndrome)

The more serious health effects, which may result in premature death or serious illness, include:

- Liver damage and cirrhosis: alcohol causes the liver to harden and inhibits its ability to filter blood. The liver performs a whole range of functions vital to life. Once it is unable to perform effectively, ill health and death are likely to follow quickly.

- Brain damage, resulting in memory loss, impaired balance and confusion.

- Mental health problems: alcohol not only aids anxiety, it also causes it and exaggerates it.

- Epilepsy, which can result from changes in brain activity caused by alcohol.

- Cancers: specifically of the liver, breast, mouth and throat.

- Diabetes: alcohol affects the liver's ability to make glucose, which is needed to manage insulin and blood sugar levels.

- Obesity: alcohol is high in calories and sugar.

- High blood pressure, which may lead to strokes.

- Hepatitis (liver inflammation).

- Sexual problems: alcohol increases impotency and infertility.

The remainder of this chapter goes to Matt to relate his chilling and emotive account of hitting absolute rock bottom with his alcoholism.

The beginning...

Although my drinking had been at what most people would consider a dangerous level for many years, I would say that the beginning of the end was 10 September 2001 – the day before 9/11 and the day that I began working at the company exporting manuals mentioned in the previous chapter. I had left the safe and familiar environment of my job at the foreign language specialist bookshop and was attempting to broaden my horizons, not realizing that the place I had chosen was, for me, just about the least appropriate position that I could have picked. When I left this job after only four months and spent six months on the dole, my drinking accelerated, and even getting what was to be my final job for several years didn't cause me to slacken the pace that I consumed alcohol. I recognize that I had been affected by depression to some degree since childhood, though I had attempted to ward it off by using humour; now it became impossible to bear, and I could no longer hold down a full-time job.

I left work and returned home anticipating the anger of my wife when she heard that I had left my job, and we would lose my income. My redundancy came as a bolt out of the blue to her, and her reaction was totally justified. Although our relationship had been going though a difficult phase, she had no real inkling of the depth of my despair, or that my drinking had reached such horrendous levels. I spent the next week more or less in bed, drinking Jack Daniels and fighting the intense blackness which was crippling my mind. I find it hard even now to take myself back to those days. They were the grimmest and most horrific days I have ever experienced. After about a month, I went to the GP and was diagnosed with clinical depression, and prescribed fluoxetine, better known as Prozac. However, due to my fear of my liver being damaged by taking this drug and having read about it on the internet, it would be another six months before I actually started taking it, a fact I hid from everyone around me. I didn't want to acknowledge the depth of the anxiety I was feeling about both my drinking and the damage I could feel I had done to myself physically as a result.

Finally I suggested to my wife that I move out, temporarily I hoped, and she acquiesced immediately, understandably but painfully from my point of view.

I moved back to live with my mother and, with the odd attempt to go cold turkey with no proper support, spent the next year drinking spirits more and more heavily. My days consisted of drinking and staring out of the window, to the despair of my family. I genuinely felt at the time that I was fighting to keep my sanity, and that my life was not worth living any more.

I felt unable to travel far from the flat, only managing to go across the road to get fresh supplies of alcohol and newspapers. I couldn't face public transport or crowds of people; this was too overwhelming for me. Once, when I attempted to use the London Underground, I had to alight at every station as I was unsure as to whether I could make it to the end of my journey. When I visited my GP in North London, I needed to be taken by my sister and her partner. I couldn't make the journey on my own, and could barely talk to the doctor. My sister did all the communicating on my behalf.

With the odd spell of sobriety achieved through sheer willpower, I was awash with strong alcohol for much of the year. At one point, I became so desperate that I strove to get myself admitted to a psychiatric unit, which I achieved after spending all day in my local A & E unit until I was seen by a qualified doctor. I spent a week in an acute psychiatric ward having an emergency detox, during the hottest spell of weather ever seen in the UK, in August 2003. Although my wife came to see me every day during my stay, these visits were some of the last occasions that I was to have contact with her. Once discharged from the unit, it was only a week before I was drinking again.

I applied for a job in a children's bookshop, and was on the point of getting it when I admitted that I had been suffering from depression and was on anti-depressants. I had decided that I wanted to be totally honest about my mental state (although not to the point of admitting to my drinking problem). By the time I arrived home, there was a phone call saying that the job had been offered to another person. This led me into my final drinking spiral from October 2003 until January 2004.

My bedroom was carpeted with empty gin bottles – literally. I slid over the glass upon getting up in the morning. I was scarcely sleeping at all. I used to drink 24 hours a day, and lie awake in bed through the night, waiting for the off licence opposite to open again. I would lie there, waiting to hear the sound of the first planes coming in to land at Heathrow Airport, which would tell me it was about 5a.m. Then I would fight the nausea and dry retching that I had every morning, as well as the terrific shivering fits and burst of sweat which ran down my back and broke out on my forehead. I dressed slowly, as any sudden movements cased a wave of sickness to sweep over me, necessitating a dash for the toilet.

I would sit on the bed, fully dressed, my knees pulled up under my chin, holding myself together until I heard the most wonderfully blissful sound: the shutters being raised on the shop selling my booze. I would wait five minutes, tell my mother I was going to get the newspapers, then dash over to get the papers, and a couple of bottles of gin to take away the severe withdrawal symptoms I was suffering.

Once back in my room, I would have a couple of swigs of gin, which gave me a wonderful feeling of relief and warmth as the terrible anxiety caused by withdrawal gradually faded away. I would top up throughout the day, existing in a warm haze of alcohol fumes and blissful euphoria. The world seemed far away, and my depression was kept at bay in the short term by the delights of drink.

This was my existence throughout the winter of 2003–4, at the age of 42. I was too ill to spend Christmas Day with my family at my sister's, and was kept from withdrawals only by my sister dropping off a bottle of whisky to help me from succumbing to fits. In fact, I had suffered from a mild attack of fitting during Christmas Day as I was lying in bed, but had not been able to contact anyone as I simply felt too ill.

That December, I was also given my first follow-up appointment by Wandsworth Council Mental Health Services. I saw the Community Alcohol Team (CAT) nurse, accompanied by my sister. My sister attempted to stress the gravity of the situation, but I just didn't appear ill enough to cause a major panic – until my blood test results were received. I was admitted to A & E as an emergency case purely due to the results of a liver function test, which had alarmed my contact on the local CAT. Gamma GT is an enzyme whose elevated level can be indicative of liver problems. The average level is 60 in a normal person, with a level of over 100 being a cause for further investigation. Mine was 2500, which was the highest that some of the medical staff had ever seen.

I was in hospital for nearly a week with liver and kidney problems. I didn't realize, until I was discharged and met my CAT nurse again, the seriousness of my condition. He told me that he had thought there was a 50/50 chance that I would not come out of hospital alive, and he proceeded to talk me through the damage I had done to my body, including my pancreas which was, in his words, 'atrophied'. It was then that I was told that I simply had to go into rehab as I might not survive another bout of drinking. This was to be funded by my local health authority. I chose a rehab from a list supplied by the CAT and awaited an appointment for an interview. I must admit that I had no idea that such help was available, and was immensely grateful for this intervention.

Once discharged from hospital, I returned home and managed to stay sober for approximately six weeks. I managed to get some support from the local services in the form of counselling from a specialist alcohol organization for one hour a week. This proved a lifeline, as I could plan my week around this hour and see it as 'this by dint of willpower'. I also had a weekly visit to an alcohol support service where I saw a counsellor, which enabled me to have an aim and a focus during the week.

The year 2004 was a turning point in my alcoholism. In January, I not only first became aware of the nature of Asperger Syndrome (of which I previously knew nothing), and how it might relate to me; I also became seriously ill with liver failure later in the year.

A BBC news items about Mark Haddon's *The Curious Incident of the Dog in the Night-time*, which included an item about Asperger Syndrome itself, alerted me to aspects of AS in which I saw myself clearly reflected. A phenomenal memory for facts and figures, often of no practical use, was one of the first. A love of routine and sameness, and reading the same book and watching the same film many, many times was another. A total lack of basic common sense was a further symptom which sounded very familiar to me, and had often been the cause of great embarrassment for me in my school and work life. A great anger that was often hard to express was one more piece of the jigsaw which seemed to fit very accurately.

However, one morning in mid-March 2004, I awoke to find the desperate depression had returned. I fought all day to not turn once again to gin as a short-term method of fighting this depression, but in the end succumbed. I felt so desperate that in the end it seemed like a choice between alcohol and suicide. I chose alcohol in the hope that I would be able to stop again before it killed me.

... The end

This was by far the heaviest drinking that I had ever done: up to three large bottles of gin per day. I could sense that I was approaching a crisis point. Nobody could drink as much gin as I was consuming without causing serious damage or death to themselves. My personal rock bottom was the day of my final drink, Sunday 4 April 2004. I had drunk two large bottles of gin and was half way through my third when I realized that something was terribly wrong. I was in no pain, but I felt the world around me growing dim, and I can distinctly remember the sensation of myself starting to go out, like a candle being extinguished. In fact, 'extinguished' is probably the best word to describe the sensation of fading away that I experienced.

I told my mother how I was feeling and she immediately phoned my brother, who came around to take me to hospital. Even then, I was so determined to have alcohol in me that I was still trying to finish the final bottle when he arrived. He took it from me and poured it away, then more or less carried me to his car.

I was taken to St George's Hospital in Tooting, where I was given a drip and had blood tests taken. I had not eaten properly for three months and was too weak to move around under my own steam, such that I needed a wheelchair to be taken around the hospital.

I was too weak even to ring the bell to notify the nurses that I needed any help, and so was unable to tell them when I needed to go to the toilet. I had to wet the bed and lie in it until the next morning. This was probably the lowest point of the entire drinking experience for me.

The next day I was put in a separate room on my own. That night I experienced horrific hallucinations and was trapped in a repeating dream which seemed never ending. To this day, I cannot recall the substance of the dream, simply the feeling that I was caught for all eternity in a repeating situation, in a loop that came around every few minutes. It was even there when I awoke. I could not escape the cycle of thoughts going through my mind. It felt like an extreme form of mental torture, and one I wouldn't wish on anybody. This was one of the experiences that gave me the impetus to remain sober, and one that I would never like to have repeated. I swore to myself that, if I got through the night, I would not put myself in a situation where I would have such a dreadful night again – I felt utterly trapped in the same visions throughout the night.

I was visited the next morning by a team of doctors on their rounds. The head doctor approached my bed and bent down, saying gently that I had to be aware I could *never* drink again. She stressed that my blood sample had been almost pure gin, a level of alcohol that would have killed any of the doctors in the room. I later found out that it was 538 mg/ml, or nearly seven times the drink/driving limit: over 400 mg/ml can be fatal in a non-drinker. I had lived and stayed conscious, which seemed to stun them even more, due to my built-in tolerance through years of heavy drinking. Most people would have been comatose with that level of alcohol in their system. I was happily sitting up and chatting to the nurses!

Once discharged again, I managed to stay sober for another six weeks until I eventually entered rehab. Two weeks after my discharge, I visited the rehab that I eventually decided on as the one for me: Aquarius, in Northampton. I was particularly impressed by the ethos of personal responsibility, and of letting the client choose whether or not to use drugs or drink alcohol, rather than using coercion. Also, I had a good feeling about the town itself, and thought that it would be a good town in which to effect a change in my life. This proved very much to be the case.

Northampton is a medium-sized market town, very compact compared to what I was used to in London, and with a much slower pace of life. I understood at a very deep level that I needed a complete change of environment in order to make the changes necessary in myself to live a life of abstinence. I perceived the town to be a place where I could slowly heal myself and learn a lot more about a new way of life, one where I could also learn more about my new understanding of AS, as I was aware that this also held the key to a productive future for myself.

Key Points

○ Whilst for some with AS, alcohol can for many years be a useful means of managing anxiety, continued excessive consumption may lead to more problems than it solves, including an increase in anxiety and other mental and physical health problems, including death.

○ The majority of adults with and without AS drink moderately with relatively few harmful effects. Drinking becomes a 'problem' when individuals continue to drink despite alcohol causing significant difficulties in their life: when drinking is no longer a 'choice' but a 'need'.

○ Those with AS may find it harder to recognize the extent of their alcohol problem.

○ Those with AS may not receive support until their alcoholism is more advanced, due to having fewer people in their social network who could alert appropriate professionals.

CHAPTER 6

DRYING OUT -
SUPPORT AND
REHABILITATION

The point has been reached where the use of alcohol is no longer an effective means of managing anxiety for the individual. For Matt, this had a high price tag; his entire life broke down and he had hit rock bottom. At this stage, the impact on family and friends, and the ability to work and function to an acceptable level are too noticeable to ignore, although many people may still not admit that there is a problem even when all around them is falling apart. Eventually, a point may come where they simply cannot ignore it. Matt's point of no return was the moment he realized that if he didn't get to hospital immediately, he would die. NHS research shows 35,400 hospital admissions for liver disease in 2004–2005 (Institute of Alcohol Studies 2006). This number has increased by over 100 per cent from the previous decade. There may be an added difficulty for people with AS in appreciating the severity of the situation due an impaired ability to engage in abstract thought and imagine events which have not yet happened. It may be that no amount of warnings from others can convince them of an impending situation (e.g. ill health or death) that they're not experiencing (i.e. they are currently still alive and well).

The treatment options, once this stage is reached, are fairly narrow, but the delivery method and ethos may vary between establishments. Some may suit individuals with AS better than others. These are reviewed briefly here. The premise of this book is that those with AS are more prone to social anxiety disorders, and that research has shown that those with social anxiety are more than twice as likely to self-medicate with alcohol. As we saw in the first chapter, alcoholism research indicates a number of factors that appear to increase the risk of addiction, including a family history of alcoholism, geographical location, income and others. This is not the arena to examine these in detail here, but confer with the notion that the more risk factors, the higher the risk. Not all those with AS or social anxiety become alcoholics, so it is not a direct causal link.

In an individual with AS and alcoholism, the alcoholism must be treated within the confines of the autistic personality. It must also be highlighted that the drinking behaviour may have been a very efficient coping strategy for such people. They drink for a very sound reason: it's the only way they know to exist in the world. Removing this protective layer against the confusions and expectations of a social world may unearth high levels of anxiety and depression. The management of anxiety must go hand in hand with the withdrawal of alcohol. It is important that support workers have a good knowledge of AS, as the perspective of the AS alcoholic may be somewhat different to a neuro-typical alcoholic. Underneath the alcoholism there will always be a person with autism who has to learn to cope with the world without the crutch of alcohol. The desire to return to alcohol as a medication against that anxiety will be particularly strong for this person. There may also need to be a programme in social skills to enable the person to feel more confident about social situations and reduce the need for the substance.

Another aspect which has been shown to benefit many people with AS is the knowledge of their condition. The more self-aware that they can become, and the greater the recognition of the limitations and advantages of their condition, the higher the levels of self-acceptance and, with it, self-esteem. Quite often, people with AS are acutely aware of being different socially, and suffer shame and feelings of inadequacy throughout their lives, although this may not be verbalized. Drinking can be a way of hiding. Learning about AS can give individuals a sense of power and control over their behaviour and reactions. For Matt, an official diagnosis, as a result of seeing a programme on TV, was a big part of his ability to remain dry, as he felt that he had an explanation for all the years of anxiety and need for predictability.

There has been no research on people with AS using alcohol services (known to the authors), so the comments and opinions here reflect personal experience and opinion rather than large-scale study. In light of this, it would be advisable to seek expert advice and take a trial-and-error approach to finding the right service for any individual. Matt provides his experience of the rehab he attended, which was a positive environment for him, although more out of luck than design: neither he nor the unit were aware of his AS at the time of his admittance. The techniques used there just happened to suit his needs and were consistent with current thinking regarding strategies to help those with AS, namely Cognitive Behavioural Therapy. This focuses on changing behaviour and is very concrete and logical, which suits the autistic mind better than more emotion-based psycho-analytic therapies.

What follows is a brief review of the range of alcoholism treatment options, including anxiety management options, followed by Matt's experience of rehab. Matt has not relapsed, but many do. The range of medication for the treatment of the anxiety and depression which often accompany AS is wide and varied, and even involves combinations of drugs which work well together. One pill does not suit all, and individuals have very differing experiences of the same type of medication, depending on how it worked for them. Specialist medical knowledge is required to determine the correct treatment for each individual. The information presented regarding medication is purely from personal experience and anecdotal remarks, but may provide a starting point in seeking appropriate help in a sea of confusing and conflicting medication options. Where we have information from those with experience it is included, but this is not to be regarded as a comprehensive guide to all medications or treatments available.

Treatment and support options

Anecdotal evidence suggests that the level and type of service and support received by any individual is a postcode lottery: it varies widely across the UK. Some people report excellent support, others none at all.

Local drug and alcohol misuse services

Most large towns and cities in the UK have services for those who require support with their addictions. These may be statutory, or staffed by trained volunteers and rely on funding to continue their services. Support offered may vary but often includes groups, counselling and provision of information, and some now also offer complementary therapies such as acupuncture, which is said to relieve cravings. Some also run education programmes for young people, to prevent alcoholism later in life. If the problem is not so severe as to lead to hospitalization or criminal activity, this may be the first point of contact when someone comes to terms with the fact that he or she needs help with his or her drinking.

Detoxification ('detox')

Some agencies and private clinics offer detoxification programmes where individuals are supported in their own homes to remain substance-free. Adequate support needs to be provided for anyone attempting detox. Medicine is prescribed that reduces the withdrawal symptoms, which are the result of stopping drinking. The most commonly used medication is chlordiazepoxide. The detox typically takes around a week, with the medication being reduced daily.

Self-help groups

The most famous of these is Alcoholics Anonymous (AA). There is no formal membership. The focus is on getting off alcohol and staying off. There are no half measures with AA: total abstinence is the goal, not moderation or controlled drinking. AA is not concerned with the why, how and what of alcoholism, it purely exists as support for the individual who recognizes that he or she has a problem. Alcoholism is seen as a medical illness, and one which has taken over the individual. There is a spiritual element to the 'Twelve Steps', which members are required to follow, but this is said not to be a religious doctrine and is open to the interpretation of members. Other self-help groups may be affiliated to local services or residential units.

I attended AA for five years. I found the services positive. I don't have a problem talking 'to' people... I was serious about my drinking problem. I had lost control. I like to be in control of my life. (Male with Asperger Syndrome)

Alternative treatments

Acupuncture, hypnosis, nutrition and relaxation are used as part of some programmes for learning to live without alcohol. These are generally part of a larger strategy and not the entire treatment. Any techniques which can maintain low stress levels may be beneficial in reducing the need for a drink.

Day services

Some agencies provide day centres where those with alcohol problems can spend time and interact with others. These centres generally do not run a structured programme or attend to the drink problem itself, but provide a safe place, especially if the individual is homeless or on a low income.

Rehabilitation centres

These take the form of residential care facilities designed to keep the individual off alcohol by means of providing specialist support. The length of stay may be 12 months or longer. Research carried out by Alcohol Concern (2006b) shows that 50 per cent of clients remain abstinent at six months after discharge from the service. The element of removing a person from his or her everyday life (and associated drinking habits and acquaintances) for an extended period and being part of a group of others experiencing the same journey seems to be part of the benefit of these centres. Approaches taken by rehabs vary; some follow the Twelve-Step programmes endorsed by Alcoholics Anonymous (AA), whilst others use Cognitive Behavioural Therapy, psychotherapy or other approaches.

- *Twelve Step programmes*: These follow the Twelve Steps of Alcoholics Anonymous, as mentioned above, which involve recognizing oneself as powerless to alcohol, and learning ways to make amends and live with sobriety. As Matt suggests later, some people with AS may struggle with the concept of an abstract 'power' as suggested in AA methodology. Many people with AS, in the author's experience, are not religious and would not subscribe to a spiritual basis for recovery. Further research is required to ascertain success rates for this group in all forms of treatment.

- *Cognitive Behavioural Therapy (CBT)*: CBT is a therapy-based form of treatment, involving a trained professional. Its rationale is that the way one thinks and perceives one's world influences the way one behaves. By providing techniques to change thoughts, one can in turn change one's behaviour. This is currently reputed to be the most effective type of therapy for those with AS (although no research is known about alcohol treatment in this group). It is a clear methodology that the person with AS may find easy to understand. The therapy does not involve re-living past experiences in order to locate cause, as in psychotherapy; the focus is on concrete behaviour rather than abstract thoughts.

- *Psychotherapy*: Psychotherapy involves talking with a trained therapist. The therapy will differ, depending on the school of thought from which the therapist comes. They may come from the perspective of psychoanalysis, using Freud's theories, where mental illness (and therefore alcoholism) is attributed to childhood conflicts; or they may come from other perspectives. Basically, these all involve discussions of feelings and looking backwards to determine causes and reasons for the drinking. There is a place for psychotherapy in working with those with AS, but this will need to be individualized. The person may find it difficult to express emotions and feelings in verbal form and the therapist may misunderstand motivations based on a potentially 'poor' performance in this type of setting. Language and comprehension differences within this client group require different methods. Assumptions made on how most people respond or react will need to be re-defined. The therapist needs a full understanding of the condition and how this has impacted on the necessity to drink, rather than assume causes from the past.

Measures of success, consequences of failure

As we have seen, the number of admissions to hospital from alcohol-related illness is growing. The consequence for those drinkers who have damaged their health irretrievably, and who are unable to maintain sobriety, will be death (as would almost certainly have been the case for Matt).

- The figures for alcohol-related deaths have more than doubled in the past decade. This equates to 8386 deaths in the UK during 2005 (Office for National Statistics 2006).

- Suicide is also connected to both social anxiety and alcohol. Eight times as many people commit suicide whilst under the influence of alcohol as without. As many as 65 per cent of suicides have been linked to excessive drinking, and up to 40 per cent of men who kill themselves have a longstanding alcohol problem. This is not to suggest that all those who commit suicide have a drink problem, although there is striking evidence that there is a big overlap between mental health conditions and problem drinking.

- The number of hospital admissions with a primary or secondary diagnosis of 'mental and behavioural disorders due to alcohol' was over 90,000 cases during 2005.

- Around 66 per cent of alcohol dependent adults entering treatment show evidence of anxiety and/or depression (Mental Health Foundation 2006). Clearly, not all of these people have AS but this certainly adds weight to the argument that even those without AS show a link between alcohol and anxiety.

Whether an alcoholic manages to remain dry depends on many factors. Staying within the treatment service is one of them. The more the individual engages with support, the better his or her chance of staying off alcohol. Alcohol Concern (2006b) research shows a progressively marked increase in several milestones as time and contact continues.

These include improved social circumstances, abstinence, improved health and more stability in housing. Abstinence increased from 25 per cent after one initial session to 78 per cent after six months. Alcohol is ever-present in our society so it is difficult for the recovering alcoholic to avoid. Having somewhere to go and speak to people who understand what they are going through seems to be a crucial part of the recovery process. Matt certainly describes this feeling in his journey through rehab. For the individual with AS, and no doubt many others, the process of stopping drinking may be only the beginning. The underlying stress, anxiety and difficulties coping with life will be all the more prominent. There would have been a comfort in drinking that is no longer available. It will be a very hard time. The understanding of these central traits is vital in order to find a suitable replacement for alcohol in these individuals. This may take the form of anti-depressant or anti-anxiety medication, relaxation techniques, stress management strategies or counselling. Relapse may occur if the newly felt emotions get too overwhelming.

When I arrived at Aquarius, a rehab in Northampton, in May 2004, I had been given an ultimatum by the alcohol services where I had been living in Wandsworth – I simply had to go into rehab or I would most likely die. The choice was mine, but it was made clear that I had gone beyond the reach of the help that local services could provide, and I would need a residential stay. An alcohol counsellor had even sketched the shape of a coffin in the air when I asked what might happen if I didn't go. There was a strong sense of relief that the decision had been taken out of my hands and that I was left with no alternative. I decided that leaving London might be of benefit, so I looked for treatment centres in different parts of the country.

Uprooting myself by moving to a new town and living for six months in a house of total strangers was as daunting to me as might be expected, especially in hindsight. A huge change in routine and lack of familiarity was guaranteed to be very stressful to somebody on the Autistic Spectrum. However, I had realized in the short period of sobriety that I had had that there was the need for a drastic change in my pattern of living and thinking to enable me to function without the support of the alcohol or tranquillizers that had underpinned my existence for so many years.

I was given the option of different kinds of rehab by the Community Alcohol Team in Wandsworth. Most of these were Twelve-Step, AA based; some involved living in part of a Christian community, which, as a non-churchgoer and non-believer in organized religion didn't appeal to me at all. I had never felt comfortable attending AA meetings in the past and felt there was the air of a cult about them. They didn't seem to be open to the ideas of anyone who challenged them. Those who advocated other methods of treatment were told that AA was the only method of staying sober that was proven to work. Mine may be an unfair assessment, but I can only express my own personal view of what I had experienced. Aquarius was described as a 'therapeutic community' with no religious connotation at all, which to me sounded welcoming and also a more rounded method of treatment than AA.

I was to discover that Aquarius used Cognitive Behavioural Therapy (CBT). This therapy aims to make one examine one's thoughts and change them if they are 'faulty', e.g. if one tends to generalize, or if small detail tends to cloud one's entire perspective. The link is made between the thoughts and feelings that may lead to addictive behaviour. By challenging these thoughts and the feelings associated with them, this behaviour can be amended. By coincidence, this seems to be the best therapy for those on the Autistic Spectrum. It is very concrete and logical, and for me there were no unexplained sections where I might have struggled to 'fill in the gap'.

I had to spend an assessment week during which I lodged in a nearby bed-and-breakfast and visited the house during the day. This enabled me to get a feel for the place and for the people already living in the house, and them for me. I attended the various therapeutic groups and saw the real sense of community and support amongst the residents.

Those wishing to enter the house as a resident had to attend a meeting where the residents were allowed to air any misgivings they might have about newcomers, and even vote not to let them into the house if they judged them to be a potential risk to the recovery of those already there. This might be due to their attitude or the sense that this rehab would not work for them.

Once in the house, the first thing I discovered was that there was a fixed routine for attending groups and doing tasks such as housework and shopping. These were pinned up in the kitchen, which I found a great help in keeping track of my week. The week was set out in a grid system, which I found easy to follow and which allowed me to maintain a picture in my head of what I needed to be doing and where I needed to be at a given time. I have brought this structure into my new life after rehab, having weekly schedules pinned up by my bed, so that I always have a picture in my mind of the days ahead. This approach helps to manage the need for predictability and structure that many with AS find so important.

The group work consisted of 'Alternatives to Drink/Drugs', levels 1 and 2 (known as ATD I and ATD II). ATD I consisted of forming short-term strategies for coping with problematic situations where using might occur. This usually involved recognizing 'triggers' for usage, such as anxiety, stress or familiar situations, and formulating alternatives, such as making a phone call, taking a bath or going for a walk – anything to fill the time when a craving strikes. Cravings are scientifically recognized as lasting around 20 minutes, so the replacement activity should last at least this long. The strategies learned in ATD I were very basic, and could be compared to putting a sticking plaster on a wound: i.e. a short-term strategy until proper assistance can be received.

The second level of therapy, or ATD II, involved the much longer-term strategy of changing one's way of thinking and perceiving problems. Residents were taught to recognize, and thus change, the way that 'faulty thinking' affects the desire to drink. Problems were to be recognized for what they were, and the real, underlying fear was to be addressed and challenged. The validity of the fear or problem was to be judged, and effective challenges as to its veracity were to be worked out.

One of the key benefits of the therapy was the highly visual nature of much of the work the groups did. Flip charts and whiteboards were much in evidence as we worked our way through the various stages of problematic situations and the different means of dealing with them. I found that there were no 'holes' or gaps in the process, which might have left me stranded this side of comprehension, as if on the edge of a ravine. We did not seem to be left to draw conclusions – each stage was thoroughly explored so that our comprehension was ensured. This is a facet of the way my thinking processes work, which I had never been able to understand about myself, and which I now understand to be typical of people with ASC. When the entire route though the recognition and treatment of the manner in which faulty thinking led to drinking was explained, without *any* gaps, I could understand perfectly. Should an item be left out, with the assumption that I would be able to bridge the gap myself, I was frozen in incomprehension. I recognized that this had been a handicap throughout my years of study at school and university, and had added to self-hatred for my perceived stupidity. I have always set a high store by intelligence in a person, and found it hard to deal with my own shortcomings in this respect.

I found the very concrete nature of the therapy worked perfectly for me. It was credible and logical, and required not a leap of faith but the ability to be realistic about the challenges I faced, and my getting a sense of proportion about my fears and anxieties.

One of the key aspects of my recovery was the way Aquarius lifted the stress from my shoulders, stress I had lived with for as long as I can remember. Money problems, always a key trigger, were simplified and could be dealt with before they overwhelmed me. In the past, letters from the bank would require the consumption of a full bottle of Jack Daniels before I could face opening them. There were always members of staff who I could turn to if there was anything which was troubling me, and there was no shame in doing so. Previously, I might have held back from asking for assistance as I had always believed that I should be able to deal with any problems in my life on my own, without troubling others. Here, asking for assistance was actively welcomed as a new way of dealing with the worries that might have led to drinking in the past. I felt a relaxation which I had never experienced before. The absence of anxiety enabled me to learn ways of coping with difficult situations in an environment unlike any I had known before.

Communal living, where everyone knew the tasks they had to perform, and where we all were learning how we needed to change in order to live without drink or drugs, was an ideal test bed for a new existence for me. I could share concerns with others, never had to carry intolerable burdens of anxiety or depression alone, and there were always others to whom I could turn.

The key point, strongly put over by the counsellors, was that we were all responsible for our own sobriety. There was no need to call on a 'Higher Power', as in AA, to keep yourself sober. The power lay within ourselves, and we just needed help to correct the faulty thinking which led to addictive behaviour. This rational and clear line of argument was wholly credible to me. I imagine that, for many people on the Autistic Spectrum who are usually quite logical, the idea of a supernatural being helping one to become sober might seem rather difficult to swallow. The idea that there are clear, easy-to-follow guidelines and simple techniques which, once internalized, can be called upon, is hugely appealing to the autistic mind. I have not looked back since, and know that there are certain lessons I have learnt so well that I can never imagine drinking alcohol again.

A structured environment, strong support and shared experience were the bedrock which enabled me to live life sober, and also to move on in learning more about my autism.

Discovering the Autistic Spectrum

Matt's experience of discovering his AS quite late in life is one shared by increasing numbers of adults. The work of Hans Asperger was not translated into English until relatively recently. Classic Autism, which typically includes a learning disability, was identified by Leo Kanner, an American, working in the 1940s – the same time as Asperger. Because English was his native language, the awareness of Kanner's autism has been far greater than that of Asperger.

Since the translation of the work of Hans Asperger, there has been an increasing number of children identified, who would previously have been labelled stupid, disruptive, schizophrenic, retarded and many other unhelpful terms. Other family members have identified themselves following the diagnosis of these children, and there has been increasing interest, information and research published, all of which has brought these Autistic Spectrum Conditions to the attention of the wider population. The internet has played a huge part in this, with individuals creating online networks and resource sites to 'spread the word'. There are many strands of research within autism and Asperger Syndrome; some seek to cure, some to celebrate, and there are many in between.

The journey for an adult who discovers later in life that he or she has significant autistic tendencies can be a long one. There may be an immediate feeling of relief to know that there has been a reason for all of the difficulties and feelings of being apart from other people. The overwhelming feeling for some is that they were not to blame after all – something they have believed all their lives. The discovery and increasing understanding of their AS is rehabilitation in itself for most individuals, and provides an opportunity to find out who they really are and what they really need. This process of self-knowledge and acceptance of self can take a long time to assimilate, maybe even a year or two. It can be a complete re-assessment of what the person knew to be true but had no idea why. This new understanding of self may enable a more manageable future.

Diagnosis

The path to a funded diagnosis in the UK requires a referral from a GP to an appropriately qualified diagnostician – typically, a clinical psychologist or psychiatrist, who maybe based at a local (or not so local) hospital, or at a specialist AS clinic. When the person being referred is an adult, this person should be experienced in working with adults, as there are some differences in diagnosing children and adults. There is a private route to the same professional if one has the funds to pay for the diagnosis. The cost in 2007 is in the realms of £1000. Matt provides further details as to the actualities of what a diagnosis may entail. Each diagnostician may have his or her other methods, but all should gather extensive information from a number of personal sources over a period of time before making a decision.

It should be noted that for some adults, obtaining an official diagnosis is not important. Once they feel that AS answers their questions about themselves, they are satisfied. To know themselves is all they need.

> I don't have a medical diagnosis of Asperger Syndrome, just a self-diagnosis. I don't need a medical diagnosis to be satisfied. The knowledge that I am not guilty is enough. It tells me there's a reason for how I think; it's not an excuse, but a reason. (Male with Asperger Syndrome)

To follow the funded route, a sympathetic and understanding GP is required to make the referral. There are reports of GPs being unaware of the condition and refusing to concede that AS may be a possibility. There are also long waiting lists for diagnosis in some areas, while some diagnosticians lack experience in working with adults, which can result in an unexpected diagnosis that the individual may feel is incorrect. Before seeking a diagnosis, it is useful to ask oneself:

- I 'know' that I have AS, but what will I do if the clinician says that I do not?
- Will I seek a second opinion (which may also concur with the first)?
- Will I have to start again with my search for who I am?
- Will I ignore the diagnosis and remain firm in my belief that I have AS?

It is also worth considering what the advantages of an official diagnosis may be. For example, these may include:

- access to services – housing, social care, etc. – where these exist
- access to welfare benefits on the grounds of disability or incapacity

- being taken seriously by family, friends and professionals
- having one's own suspicions 'officially' verified.

The decision to seek a diagnosis is a personal one and should be considered carefully, perhaps in discussion with others. It is also worth doing some research on what options and services will be available in the local area, as this can vary greatly. Improvements in availability and consistency of adult diagnostic services is badly needed to ensure that individuals have faith in the diagnosis that they receive, and also that they are guaranteed some follow-up support after it is made.

After the diagnosis, there is often the natural expectation that some on-going support will follow. Unfortunately, this is often not the case, as adult, specialist AS support is rare (in the UK). The most prolific source of information on AS in adulthood is the internet, with its numerous resources, groups and forums where individuals, family members and professionals are able to learn about themselves and each other. There are some funded services, but these are financially stretched and may have waiting lists. There is also some private provision in the form of counselling or coaching support, but this can be costly.

It was only four months since I had first made the connection between myself and Asperger Syndrome, and I was still very keen to do as much research into the condition whilst in rehab as I possibly could. Luckily, the main therapeutic room also had a computer with internet access for the residents, and this allowed me to delve more deeply into the condition.

The more research I did, the more excited I became, as I recognized myself in much of what I read. I began to get a picture of myself as someone with a different way of thinking, not simply someone who was sometimes stupid and sometimes smart, but never sure exactly how I was going to be in any given situation.

The anger which was always just below the surface, and which had caused me so many problems in my relationships, was described there. The love of routine, watching the same films, reading the same books many times in a row, which had before seemed inexplicable, now fitted a pattern. The phenomenal memory for the exact date of things that had been evident even in my childhood, and which I could neither explain nor justify when other, more important, information was not retained, again made sense. The total lack of common sense that had driven my father to distraction, and which had caused me much embarrassment in some of the jobs I had in the past, was part of the syndrome. I remember that the dread of anticipating any practical task to be done was one source of my anxiety, and now I understood the root cause.

I had read a book by Maxine Aston, an Asperger Syndrome relationship expert, and contacted her through her website to arrange a consultation. My family supported me yet again by paying for this consultation. Her practice was a short train ride away, and this session was one of the most exhilarating experiences of my life. I chatted to her for around 45 minutes, and she said that it did seem very likely that I was mildly autistic. I remember thinking that finally I might have found an explanation for the difficulties that, while not always obvious to others, I carried around with me everywhere. Subsequent visits built up a more complete picture for me of the link between my experience and autism. One of the most striking revelations I had was when describing my reaction to seeing someone come along and perform a simple task, such as operating a piece of equipment, which I had been unable to do. Maxine Aston asked me to describe what I saw when people did this, and I distinctly recall the vision coming to me of a magic trick being performed: an illusion that I could not decipher.

Encouraged by this confirmation of the belief in my condition, I contacted the Northamptonshire Society for Autism. They gave me the details of a local hospital unit I could approach if I sought a diagnosis of Asperger Syndrome. I was truly fortunate to have chosen a rehab in Northampton; this county has one of very few centres in the UK where adults on the Autistic Spectrum can hope to get a diagnosis of their condition. All I needed to do was ask my GP for a referral. I was blessed with a sympathetic doctor, which is not the case for many adults who struggle to be heard by the medical profession. I managed to get my case referred, although I still had to wait three months before I was contacted by the unit. I was sent a sheaf of questionnaires to be completed by myself and my family, in order to give the psychologist as complete a picture of my background as possible. Over the next two months or so, I attended a clinic for a series of interviews, and had to supply my school reports to give an idea of my educational history. The most daunting aspect was a series of tests which looked at my general knowledge, visual, spatial and verbal abilities, as well as my capacity for problem-solving.

I was finally given a diagnosis of PDD-NOS (Pervasive Developmental Disorder Not Otherwise Specified). This is a diagnosis made when the patient either has all the features needed for a diagnosis of AS, but not to the necessary degree, or where not all of the features are present, but enough are to warrant a diagnosis of PDD-NOS.

I was overjoyed to receive this diagnosis. I was aware at a very profound level that I had some mild form of autism, and that this explained the problems, as well as some of the successes, that I had experienced in my life. I had read books about AS and caught myself continually nodding and saying 'that's me!' I did much research online and it became clear to me that the stress and anxiety side of ASC made sense of the continual underlying sensation of dread I had when simply going about my everyday life. I had often thought that I would like to have an operation to remove my adrenal glands, if it were possible, simply to stop this nameless terror which filled my waking thoughts.

As I learned new life skills at rehab, such as planning my days in a more methodical way, getting problems into proportion, and not catastrophizing negative situations so that I felt swamped by them, other, more positive, aspects of this diagnosis became obvious to me. I had very definite skills which had stood me in good stead whilst working in bookshops for the previous 20 years.

My phenomenal memory had enabled me to run both an art bookshop when I had no previous knowledge of contemporary art, as well as a department dealing in some highly obscure languages in the largest language bookshop in the UK, again when I had no prior experience in this field. Being able to recall book details without consulting my computer vastly sped up my capacity to deal with customer enquiries. My general knowledge enabled me to make links between countries, languages and suppliers of books, which made ordering titles much more efficient. I was very good at research details, and I found myself becoming fascinated by the geographical and historical background of which languages were spoken where, and why. This was, of course, where my work became a special interest, and I was now thrilled to see the positive elements of having an autistic mind.

I obtained a position volunteering at the Northamptonshire Society for Autism as a part-time office worker. Here I not only learnt much more about the different kinds of problems faced by those on the Autistic Spectrum, but also met others who had first-hand experience of the condition, usually with close relatives. This, combined with my deep interest in understanding the root causes of substance misuse, led me to investigate the connection between alcoholism/substance misuse and the intense anxiety often suffered by people with Asperger Syndrome. I knew I had originally used alcohol as a readily available tranquilliser in situations of great apprehension: not just difficult social situations either, but any situation involving authority figures or money problems. In these sorts of situations, my mind would freeze up and I would feel totally incapable of interacting with anybody. I noticed that I would feel exactly the same in these situations as I did when asked to perform practical tasks. I would feel totally useless, yet I knew that I had a great wealth of knowledge, which had enabled me to hold down some very good jobs in bookshops.

There are various aspects of my time in rehab which I believe coalesced to create the perfect environment for me to learn long-term lessons about sobriety. Being able to call on others for support, even in the middle of the night, was a wonderful safety net for someone prone to dwelling on worries and letting anxiety build until alcohol seemed the only viable solution. Sharing my experiences with others who had often been through even tougher times, involving prison and the death of close family members, showed me, in a believable way, that I was not alone in my troubles. Having real-life examples made so much more of an impression on me than any abstract notion of the misfortunes of others ever could have done.

Weekly one-to-one therapy enabled me to build up a trusting relationship with somebody who had no preconceptions about me, and who could give me expert, impartial advice about aspects of my life which I had not been able to discuss properly before. Even such small matters as sitting around a table for a communal meal every evening was a wonderful experience for someone who had cut himself off from others. Towards the end of my drinking, I had not eaten any solid food for some time, subsisting almost exclusively on gin. I discovered that my appetite returned with a vengeance and from barely eating at all, I was ravenous at mealtimes. This is typical of the experience of many alcoholics, I have discovered.

Having been born and bred in London, I had always maintained that I could never live anywhere else. However, I found that life in a medium-sized town, such as Northampton, was far more relaxed and manageable than in a massive metropolis like London. Travel by foot was my usual method, since there was scarcely any part of town I couldn't reach in this way. All the agencies and shops which I needed were near the centre of town. The pace of life is much slower, and it was quite a culture shock to return to London for visits and to be reminded of the crowds in the streets and the speed at which everyone moves there. Moving around Brighton, where I now live, is a similar experience to living in Northampton, in that it is a much more manageable town for me to be in: less stressful, more predictable travel-wise, and with a way of life more suited than London to someone with AS, in my opinion.

Much of my drinking in London was done before or during lengthy journeys by bus or tube train. I have realized that these were incredibly stressful journeys for me. I believe that I was subconsciously anxious about any disruption on the journey, and being stranded in a part of London without being sure of how to get home. I was also anxious about being involved in any trouble or violence whilst travelling across London. I have never really thought about this before, but I am aware now that my autistic thinking led me to be enormously stressed about unforeseeable events whilst travelling. To most people, this might seem highly unusual. To somebody on the Autistic Spectrum, it can be as natural as breathing.

Support from friends and family

Those with AS may have small social networks and not be able to call upon the support of friends to help them through this difficult time. To establish a new life without alcohol is difficult if the person is to remain socially isolated. It is important that some support network is in place to help to prevent a return to old drinking behaviour as a means to manage loneliness and feelings of exclusion or not 'fitting in'.

Even whilst I was drinking, my family had never stopped supporting me, even though they must have despaired at the level of my alcohol consumption and at the effect it had on me. I couldn't have achieved all that I have without this unconditional support of my mother, sister, brother and good friends. Knowing that whatever I had done in the past, they had not abandoned me, and that they thought that I was worth standing by gave me enormous energy and enabled me to get through very tough times. The encouragement and support of those close to you are of utmost importance in the rehab process, in my opinion. Although we were always told to remember that we were in recovery for our own sake and not for anybody else's, to be praised by loved ones for what we had achieved, and encouraged to carry on, were of incalculable help in keeping us going.

I was a very unpleasant and sarcastic person before, and I am aware that my anger was exacerbated by the alcohol. I was very interested to learn that anger is often part of Asperger Syndrome; I am aware that I have a ferocious temper, which I almost never let off the leash, for fear of not being able to control it. I alienated many people, including various partners, and I am a much more content person now I am sober.

Coming out the other side

I am still taking the anti-depressant fluoxetine, and other medication (beta-blockers) to prevent blood vessels in my stomach from haemorrhaging as a result of the cirrhosis I now have. I have since learnt that this combination of the group of drugs known as SSRIs, including fluoxetine, and beta-blockers is considered by many to be an ideal combination to deal with the obsessive behaviours and extreme anxiety endemic in many of those with AS. The noted autism expert Temple Grandin believes that the intense, all-pervading anxiety of those on the spectrum is helped immeasurably by this kind of medication.

Having completed six months of rehab in the main house, I spent another ten months in supported housing nearby. I was given more freedom here to do some voluntary work, and to live a more independent life. I still attended group and individual therapy sessions in the main rehab, but I was gradually becoming more independent. Eventually I became aware that the lessons I had learnt at rehab were of use everywhere, and I didn't need to stay in the comfortable secure cocoon as I had thought I might.

Key Points

- ○ The more support that a person engages with, the lower his or her chance of relapsing into alcohol consumption.

- ○ Realization and diagnosis of AS can be a large part of the alcoholism recovery process.

- ○ It is important that professionals working with those with alcoholism have a good knowledge and understanding of AS in order to provide appropriate communication and support.

- ○ Appropriate treatment options for those with AS are important in supporting recovery.

- ○ Cognitive Behavioural Therapy is seen to be beneficial to those with AS for treating anxiety.

CHAPTER 7

LIFE BEYOND THE BOOZE - RECOVERING AUTISTIC ALCOHOLIC

Enough of this doom and gloom! There is an alternative existence for those who get appropriate treatment and support. In this final chapter, we would like to consider the strategies and approaches that a person with AS may take to support a stress-free and successful life without alcohol, or any other artificial means of anxiety suppressant. One of my favourite things that Matt says when he describes how he is able to simply not get stressed by things which previously would have sent him heading for the bottle, is: 'It's like my give-a-shit nerve has been severed'!

I can honestly say that my life has been utterly been transformed by two things: the wonderful treatment I received at the rehab in Northampton, and the way I now understand myself in the wake of receiving my diagnosis. My chief fear upon leaving Aquarius was that I would not be able to take all the lessons I had learnt there with me, and that I would be prone to repeating all the errors of thinking that I had committed whilst I was drinking. However, I had internalized the lessons so well, and I had learnt a brand new way of being to such an extent, that I have weathered quite a few storms in my personal life without resorting to alcohol.

Whilst in rehab, I decided that I might like to try studying again, after a gap of more than 20 years, rather than plunge straight back into the world of work. I had greatly enjoyed my time volunteering at the medical library and decided to try my hand at training to be a librarian. Ironically, this was a career which I had considered when in my teens, but had been dissuaded from pursuing by my family and my teachers who thought that it was too 'dull' a career choice for me to make at such an age. A friend recommended a course at the University of Brighton, which looked ideal. I applied, was interviewed and got a place. I found that having access to a computer made the whole process a lot less stressful than it would have been previously. I didn't have to make many telephone calls or pay a lot of visits in order to arrange the next stage of my life; it could be done online to a large extent.

For the first time I also discovered some of the benefits of disclosure of my diagnosis. I mentioned my diagnosis on my application form and was immediately given an appointment with the disability officer. I was given an amazing amount of help, both in materials and in counselling. I was also given a room in a mature students' flat on campus, which also helped me to adjust to life after rehab, as the responsibilities upon me were limited – bills were paid for me and I just had to look after myself.

Once I began studying, I immediately began to struggle. I had elected to do an MA in Information Studies in one year; I soon found that I had taken on a task which I was not mentally prepared for. Going straight from rehab to an MA was something I chose to do to prove to others in my life, such as friends and family, that I was worth something. I am now aware that this just wasn't necessary, and that a simpler life – one in which I can be myself and take care of myself – is by far the most desirable way to live.

Instead of struggling on and getting more and more depressed, I simply told the lecturers that I had decided to go part-time, then I withdrew from the course altogether. I felt a huge wave of relief wash over me upon making this decision. This was a whole new way of approaching problem-solving for me. Instead of forcing myself to do something that was making me miserable, I chose to change direction, ask for help and look around before deciding what to do with my life. In the past, I would probably have carried on doing the course and have used alcohol to help me do something which was not making me happy, which I now recognize as a strong character trait on my part. Problems in my professional and personal life were plastered over with the liberal use of excess alcohol. I could cope with genuine misery and inner discomfort as long as alcohol was there to prevent me from getting in touch with my true feelings.

At the same time, I was aware that my new self-knowledge as someone on the Autistic Spectrum allowed me to be much more forgiving of myself when I made mistakes in social situations, or if I had problems following instructions or encountered difficulties in any of the other facets of life which had been problematic for me in the past.

Instead of losing my temper with myself and utterly seething with rage at my own stupidity and incompetence, I simply shrugged and told myself that I was not being deliberately obtuse and it was just another way of being. I have problems with comprehending some parts of the world around me; it isn't my fault and I should simply get on with living my life in the best way that I possibly can.

Embracing the autistic self

One of the keys to maintaining good mental health and well-being, for anyone, is a firm knowledge and understanding of who one is and what one's strengths and limitations are. This is especially important for those with AS, as they do see the world differently than most people and need a strong sense of self to be able to assert their needs, whilst also trying to appreciate that others are quite likely to have a whole different perspective – which can be very hard to do or imagine.

The key to gaining this self-awareness lies in learning as much as possible about your condition. There is a lot of information on all aspects of autism in books, and online, through message boards, forums and research sites. Allowing yourself to absorb as many perspectives and views of autism as you can helps to get a solid sense of the community to which you belong. This self-understanding also helps to get a clearer idea of your strengths and limitations. Years of needing alcohol in order to get through the day should be enough of a clue to realize that in order not to return to drinking, serious changes need to be made. Life must be on your own terms, to protect yourself from the stress that led to the drinking, which will in turn eventually lead to ill health.

> Since I have stopped drinking, my autistic traits have come much more strongly to the fore than at any time while I was drinking. I have found myself to be much less focused and more easily distracted by anything which catches my interest. I permit myself to be obsessed by certain television programmes and routines, such as watching *Most Haunted* every night, and visiting Starbucks for coffee (and for the same actual drink) every day. I am aware now that visiting my local pub when I was drinking was as much for the feeling of familiarity and security as for the alcohol. I could simply have drunk at home, but it was the combination of the place as well as the availability of alcohol which was the key to this particular habit. I also find that my mind 'freezes' a lot more now when confronted with a problem than it did before, simply because I allow it to do so. In order to avoid anxiety, I permit myself to fail and do not harangue myself inside like I did before when I drank. My self-hatred and anger were overwhelming; now I am much more serene internally. I am doubtless a less effective manager than before, but a much nicer person to be around – and to be.

Relationships

The presence of a relationship in the life of the person with AS is potentially another stress-inducing factor. This is not necessarily due to any specific difficulties within the relationship; but merely having to consider the needs of a partner, and respond to these, creates a requirement for thought and effort, which comes at a price, draining the person's already limited resources. For someone who is recovering from a drink problem, care must be taken when beginning a new relationship to maintain low anxiety and stress levels.

The kind of relationship which could be successful for someone with AS will need to fulfil certain specifications. Obviously, there are some lasting relationships that have none of these pre-requisites, but they may be more stressful and expend more of the person's emotional capacity. The most important thing for recovering alcoholics to remember is that they must not put themselves into any situation where there may be a risk of returning to drinking behaviour. The relationship is only secondary to the sobriety of the individual. Any partner must be fully aware of this danger and appreciate that individuals with AS must put their own safety before anything else.

Sharing part of one's life with a partner is a desire for many people and can meet needs for companionship, sex, affection and care, as long as these benefits are not overshadowed by the difficulties of trying to work out the needs of someone other than oneself. Living separately may be the answer to some of these issues, allowing plenty of time alone for the person with AS and also time away for the partner, who may find the relationship somewhat tiring. The following are points that the couple may find helpful to consider:

Both partners need to:

- have a full and extensive understanding about AS, and its impact on the individual

- understand that neither partner is 'wrong', just 'different'

- communicate openly and honestly about the needs and habits of both partners; assumptions of mind-reading by either partner are unlikely to be successful and should be avoided

- communicate about matters such as physical touch and other sensory issues, the expression of feelings and emotions and how to read non-verbal signals, and routines which are non-negotiable

- understand that, in order to get his or her own needs met, each partner must provide what the other partner wants

- trust that neither partner would ask for something if he or she did not need it (regardless of whether he or she understands the reason for asking)

- be aware of each partner's overload level, and ensure that they have escape plans to manage this before danger levels of stress are reached.

The non-AS partner needs to:

- appreciate that care, love and affection may be shown in different ways by a person with AS – rather than believing that these qualities don't exist at all, which is generally not the case

- be aware of his or her role as translator to the social world, and thus feel a sense of responsibility for the AS partner

- trust that the AS partner is giving and doing as much as he or she can

- be aware that criticism is often taken very badly by those with AS due to a lifetime of awareness that they are unable to 'get it right'

- communicate difficult issues using calm, unemotional language, which will assist the AS partner in hearing and understanding what is being said.

- develop a thick skin – to cope with the brutal honesty!

- maintain his or her own social interests and activities and not rely on the partner, who may be unable or unwilling to meet these needs

- consider the value of support from others in similar relationships via online groups and forums and by reading literature in the AS relationship field (Aston 2003; Hendrickx and Newton 2007; Hendrickx 2008; Slater-Walker and Slater-Walker 2003; Stanford 2003).

The partner with AS needs to:

- be willing to compromise and meet the needs of his or her partner, even when this feels difficult

- clearly explain his or her motivations for behaviour (e.g. withdrawal and solitude) to allow the partner to understand that it is not a personal rejection.

Keith Newton (Hendrickx and Newton 2007) sums up his advice for those with AS in relationships: 'Do whatever you can for your partner – and do it often!'

There are many differences to having a partner with AS, and some of these are very positive. The partner with AS may:

- lack duplicity; less developed empathy skills can mean that some people with AS find lying and deceit difficult, as this involves putting oneself into another person's position in order to predict what he or she will believe. Some have said that working out what's going on in their own head is hard enough, without trying to work out someone else's thoughts!

- have extensive knowledge in certain subjects, which makes for interesting conversation (especially if the partner shares those interests)

- be good looking with angelic, symmetrical faces (Attwood 2006)

- be solid and reliable; they tend to do what they say they will do, as they dislike unpredictability and change

- be loyal; if the relationship meets the person's needs, it would be illogical to leave it!

- be gentle (especially men with AS); some women find this different and appealing.

I started seeing women, having some short-term relationships, and found that I was capable of a rounded life without the crutch of alcohol. I even experienced the one thing that I was dreading, the end of a relationship, which I had always coped with previously by numbing my pain with booze. That was simply not an option for me now, so I let myself experience the feelings of loss and depression, anger and hopelessness, knowing that I was being true to myself, and that I would be a stronger person for proving to myself that I could cope without artificial aids.

I am not in a relationship at the moment, as I realize that I am not ready to make the sacrifices in my lifestyle that are necessary for a mature, sharing relationship. I am too happy just to please myself and to do whatever I like, on a whim, without having to explain or justify myself to a partner. I do miss the closeness and sharing which goes with being part of a couple, but accept that I may never meet a person who will accept me as I am and with whom I will feel totally at ease.

Socializing, friendships and social situations

It can be easy for someone with AS to imagine that everyone else is having a full and active social life with drinks, lunches and evenings out together, and assume that he or she is the only one who is not included in this. The media portrays people in large groups of friends having a good time. I suspect that most people do not have an existence like that shown on TV and in films, and many people have very small social circles. It is important to try and find the level of social interaction which suits the individual, regardless of what society says is 'normal'. Many people with AS find groups difficult and prefer to meet friends on a one-to-one basis. The more people present in a group, the more non-verbal communication and social cues to be fathomed, which can cause stress and exhaustion. One or two trusted people can aid the process of social interaction and guide the person when he or she feels confused about what is expected. This requires the person with AS to be very honest about the condition and to admit when help is required. This can be difficult to do, but may produce more beneficial results than not telling anyone and taking the risk of being misunderstood, appearing rude or being excluded – and the individual not realizing what he or she has done to engender this reaction.

I tend to pass the time wandering about town, reading papers, drinking coffee and people-watching in cafes. I can contact people and arrange to speak or write to them, but there is no obligation on my part to do so. I am a totally free agent and I find that this works incredibly well for me. The idea that I might be subject to someone else's wishes makes me cringe inside. I think I am getting to know myself really well, and I am very content to do this on my own and without communicating very much with others. I can easily arrange to see any one of my small circle of friends. I prefer not to mix my friendships too much – I see them as quite separate beings, not part of a larger community of people who are my acquaintances.

I look forward to my arrangements to meet up with people for meals or to go and see a film. They provide a shape to my week, along with my work time, and I have learnt how a good routine makes time fly past for me, and stops me from dwelling on any of the things I might regret about the past.

I don't really socialize after work, in the sense of going to the pub with my workmates. I will watch films with them, but am happy to go off and do my own thing afterwards.

I have found that I have rediscovered feelings that I haven't experienced since I was a child. I take the greatest pleasure in the smallest things in my life. A cup of coffee whilst reading a newspaper, the wind blowing gently under a blue sky, the sound of birdsong, and the crash and hiss of the tide against the beach. These give me the greatest feeling of contentment and peace that I can remember in my entire adult life.

I understand that life may not always be so idyllic for me, and that problems and anxieties are bound to intrude at some point. However, I have learnt new strategies for coping with anxiety, and have gained a sense of perspective through experiencing the difficulties of the past few years. In addition, I understand that I have the support of my family and many wonderful friends, many of whom I didn't know before the turbulent times. If I can talk about the chief benefit of all the bad times, it is the opportunity it has given me to meet so many new people who are now an integral part of my life.

Employment

As with relationships and other aspects of life with AS, a solution needs to be found which meets the limitations and skills of the individual without needing to resort to previous, unhealthy coping behaviours, such as alcohol. Employment support agencies may be helpful in deciding which jobs may be appropriate, and in constructing a new CV, especially if the person has been unemployed for some time. Making the decision as to whether to disclose alcoholism or AS is a tough one. Legislation is in place to ensure that each individual is considered for work on his or her merits, but sadly, many people with disabilities are cynical and untrusting of employers, who they feel may exclude them because they perceive them to be difficult to accommodate, or may require too much time off. The disadvantage of choosing not to disclose a condition is that if issues do arise that the person struggles to manage, it will be more difficult for the employer to respond appropriately and quickly. Some who have not disclosed feel that their only option is to leave the job; or they may be fired because they have not been able to stipulate the conditions they need in order to be successful. The consequences of this are not only that the individual has lost income and may build up a poor work record, but that self-esteem and motivation may suffer, thus reducing the ability to go and try again to find suitable employment.

Matt used voluntary work as a stepping stone into employment during his time in rehab, and this can be a really useful place to begin building skills and confidence, and also to think about what kind of work would be most enjoyable and manageable. For people with AS, who can be quite focused on specific interests, and less motivated to engage in activities which they perceive to be of little personal benefit, it is vital to find a job or placement that fully fits with their interests, skills and motivators.

I found the ideal way back into the world of work almost by accident. I applied for a job at a bookshop, where the only positions were part-time. This had never occurred to me as a compromise between not working at all and working full-time. I had only thought of work on an all-or-nothing basis – once again, an example of extremely black-and-white thinking. I found that this suited me perfectly, allowing me time to follow my other pursuits, such as giving talks about my experiences, as well as writing this book! In addition, it gave me breaks from work where I could do things I had never done before, such as allowing myself to bask in the simple pleasures of life. I enjoyed walking by the sea, appreciating the different seasons, window shopping and allowing myself to people-watch whilst sitting in cafes. This may sound like 'dropping out' of conventional day-to-day life, and I agree that this is true to a certain extent. I have gone though a time of great misery, illness and sadness, and have no qualms about allowing myself to enjoy life on my own terms. I can just about afford to live in this way, and it has served me very well in my chief goal in life, namely long-term sobriety.

When I encounter problems at work, which previously might have made me burn with shame at my own perceived stupidity, and cringe under the weight of my worthlessness (as I saw it at the time), I simply shrug and refuse to put any pressure on myself. I am aware of the discrepancy between the things that I can do easily and those which I find problematic. Recall of information comes easily to me and enables me to make connections between subjects that others may not have considered, as their brains don't function in the same way.

By the same token, I struggle when given a task involving creativity and imagination, such as making a display of books that customers might find attractive, thus encouraging them to buy. When I am shown an example by a member of staff, I struggle to understand what it is that makes it succeed. This is also an aspect when it comes to questions of fashion or interior design. I have no idea why one look is good and another is not. It seems totally arbitrary – one person's choice – and there seems to me to be no logical reason why this person's taste should be given more weight than another's in something so vague and tenuous.

Strategies

I am intensely aware of potential triggers which may lead me back to drinking again. Some of the key ones are financial problems and stress over meeting obligations relating to money. Sometimes being in familiar situations where I used to drink (attending parties, being in a pub, watching a football match) can be extremely tempting for me. I can feel the old mindset slipping back into place, along with the thought 'Why can everyone else drink and I can't?' I can spot the early warning signals extremely early, as I was taught to do in rehab, along with various coping mechanisms. Dealing with issues such as housing or bank loans at an early stage, when problems are much easier to resolve, is one of them. Consciously avoiding people who may be problematic (ex-partners, or friends with whom I may find difficult feelings coming to the surface) is another key skill that I have learnt. Nobody is worth risking my life for (as I would be doing if I ever touch alcohol again), and I must never lose sight of how bad things were for me and those around me at the very height of my drinking.

Understanding that I have AS makes it easier for me to understand myself, and explains many of the problems and questions I have had all my life. It takes a massive weight off my shoulders, such as the feeling of inadequacy and of not fulfilling the expectations of others (which had always seemed so unimportant and stupid to me; now I understand why I felt this way).

Support and strategies for professionals

Specialist support for adults with Asperger Syndrome and other so-called 'high-functioning' Autistic Spectrum Conditions is varied and intermittent, with some areas having better coverage than others. In general, it can be said that it is poor and non-existent in most areas of the UK, especially for those without an official diagnosis – which in itself is hard to access for many.

For those working in the alcohol or substance misuse field, the most vital requirement is a good knowledge of autistic conditions and how they may exhibit and impact on an individual. Ideally, this would be through training, reading and talking to those with the condition about their experiences in order to gain a full knowledge.

All staff should be aware of the characteristics of social anxiety and, bearing in mind the large overlap between autism and anxiety, and anxiety and alcoholism, should be aware of typical behaviour and life history which may suggest AS. Diagnosis can only be carried out by a qualified professional, but often a support worker may be the first person to make this very important connection, which may lead to the individual receiving appropriate support, diagnosis and provision.

Every person affected by AS will experience his or her condition differently, and unfortunately for staff there is no one-size-fits-all strategy which will work for everyone. It is a case of getting to know individuals and how AS impacts on them, and working within these parameters to find a way that suits their needs: an individualistic, person-centred approach.

A knowledge of AS is essential when planning strategies and means of working with those with the condition, as it guides the type of methods which are likely to fit with the way the AS brain functions. Methods that may be used include:

- Provision of a set timetable of activity which is fairly static and only changes with prior warning; this suits the person's preference for structure and routine.

- Small group or one-to-one working; large groups can be very stressful.

- Consistency of staff; the person may prefer to work with only one member of staff and not be able to change easily.

- Consistency of approach, such that all workers communicate and work with the person in the same way.

- Written and visual timetables and instructions, so that there isn't reliance on verbal instructions alone.

- Realistic timescales; it may take a long time for the person to move forward to new behaviour, so quick progress is not to be expected. New suggestions and changes to existing behaviour patterns may cause extreme anxiety and need to be introduced slowly with as much support as required.

- Clear, preferably written, consequences of non-attendance/ non-compliance etc. These may need to be explicitly spelled out. The person may find it hard to make the mental leaps required to comprehend that failure to attend an appointment may lead, via a number of steps, to the loss of his or her benefit, home or access to a child, for example.

- Acting as a social guide and interpreter and translating the behaviour of others, so that the person can identify where misunderstanding and conflict has arisen unintentionally. Social skills training may be necessary to enable more confident interactions and thus minimize the risk of returning to drinking.

- Throwing out all assumptions as to why the person behaves in a particular way based on your own perspective; it may be very different. Prepare to be amazed!

- Minimizing anxiety – the most important factor. If the person has been using alcohol to self-medicate anxiety, it is essential that the treatment or support process does not add to this stress and lead to continued, or a return to, drinking behaviour.

- Teaching a knowledge and acceptance of self by being accepting of the person's right to think differently.

- Considering all interventions from the perspective of AS.

- Uncovering the true motivating factors and rewards or pay-offs for the individual; these may not be the same as for others.

Key Points

○ Minimizing drinking triggers is the major priority for those with AS and alcoholism.

○ Recovering alcoholics with AS need to build a life which enables them to manage their AS and minimize anxiety.

○ The expectations of others may be unrealistic and dangerous to a person with AS and alcoholism.

○ It is important for those with AS to learn about their condition and develop a strong sense of self-acceptance.

○ Anyone working or living with someone with AS should have a good knowledge of the condition and its implications to ensure that service provision is appropriate to the condition.

○ On-going support and understanding from friends, family, employers and support staff is vital in ensuring continued abstinence and good mental health.

CONCLUSION

So, what can we conclude from looking at the factors involved in both having AS and drinking alcohol to excess?

We suggest that the anxiety which is prevalent in many with AS could be managed to some degree by drinking alcohol. Alcohol is used by many 'normal' individuals as a means to aid social interaction, so would be even more essential to those with a disadvantage in this area.

Due to the only recent 'discovery' of the higher functioning autistic conditions in the English language, there may well be a number of people who are currently known as 'alcoholics', but may also be unidentified as individuals with autistic characteristics. Some of these people may not have reacted well to traditional methods of treatment for their alcoholism because they have either not addressed the underlying differences which have contributed to it, or the treatment method does not suit their autistic needs.

The possibility that someone can be both alcoholic and autistic needs to be recognized in both autism and substance misuse services, and a greater understanding of both fields established. By doing so, we may help to prevent the alcoholism taking hold, or support alcoholics with autism in understanding the reasons for their anxiety and inability to cope with the world. In both cases, a better prognosis both physically and emotionally is a real possibility.

Matt's experiences are a clear demonstration of a 'before and after AS' life. The fact that he has been able to build an entirely new life without alcohol, even though he himself is still the same person with his AS and all the stress that it brings, is a story of hope for others heading down the same road. Yes, having AS can make life more difficult at times, but knowing why seems to make a huge difference in being able to cope. Being an alcoholic as a means to manage unknown autism is really no long-term coping strategy; it is a death sentence. As professionals and family members, we have a responsibility to ensure that alcoholism is not the only route for individuals such as Matt.

The key to helping prevent this combination of conditions is better, earlier and more easily available diagnosis of AS for adults, combined with real, in-depth understanding and knowledge of this condition for all concerned. If we can tackle the issues of anxiety earlier in childhood through better provision for those with AS, then perhaps we could avoid some of the later repercussions.

> The main point I would like to get across is that it is *never* too late to change your life if you are unhappy with your addiction and wish to gain self-knowledge. I was 43 when I began to make all the changes in my life, and also when I first gained any awareness of what Asperger Syndrome actually meant for those with the condition. From being lost in the depths of addiction and depression, I am now living a life I couldn't have imagined. I enjoy every aspect of life: relationships, appreciating my environment, and simply the joy of being alive instead of merely existing.
>
> Looking back on my life, a lot makes sense in hindsight. I can honestly say that I have had many good times that outweigh the bad, and if I was given a chance to relive my life, I wouldn't like to be any different from how I am. In fact, as I often say to people who ask, I can't understand why more people don't want to be like me!
>
> I owe an enormous debt of gratitude to my family and friends who never gave up on me, even when they may have been exasperated by my behaviour. I am also grateful in a way not easily expressed to the staff at Aquarius in Northampton, along with those I met there who, like me, had come to the end of one road, and were looking to start afresh. Simply put, they gave me the tools to totally rebuild and transform my life. I will never forget this gift, and I will always try to live up to it.

REFERENCES

Abrams, K., Kushner, M.G., Medina, K., Voight, A. (2002) 'Self-administration of alcohol before and after public speaking challenge by individuals with social phobia.' *Psychology of Addictive Behaviours 16*, 2, 121–128.

Addaction (2008) 'The Financial Costs of Addiction – A Briefing on the Costs of the UK's drug problem.' Available at www.addaction.org.uk/Briefing-financialcostsofaddiction.pdf, accessed on 11 April 2008.

Alcohol Concern (2006a) 'Impact of alcohol problems on the workplace.' *Acquire Information and Research Bulletin, Winter Edition*, pp.i–vii.

Alcohol Concern (2006b) *Alcohol Treatment Outcomes and Options*. London: Alcohol Concern.

American Psychiatric Association (APA) (1994) *Diagnostic and Statistical Manual of Mental Disorders*, 4th Edition. Washington, DC: American Psychiatric Association.

Aston, M. (2003) *Asperger's in Love*. London: Jessica Kingsley Publishers.

Attwood, T. (2006) *The Complete Guide to Asperger's Syndrome*. London: Jessica Kingsley Publishers.

Barnard, J. Harvey, V., Prior, A. and Potter, D. (2001) *Ignored or Ineligible? The Reality for Adults with Autism Spectrum Disorders*. London: The National Autistic Society.

Berney, T. (2004) 'Asperger Syndrome from childhood into adulthood.' *Advances in Psychiatric Treatment 10*, 341–351.

Conger, J.J. (1956) 'Reinforcement theory and the dynamics of alcoholism.' *Quarterly Journal of Studies in Alcohol 12*, 1–49.

Department of Health (2007) *Young People and Alcohol*. London: Department of Health. Available at www.wiredforhealth.gov.uk/cat.php?catid=865&docid=7075, accessed on 13 February 2008.

Foisy, M., Kornreich, C., Petiau, C., Parez, A. *et al.* (2007) 'Impaired emotional facial expression recognition in alcoholics: Are these deficits specific to emotional cues?' *Psychiatry Research 150*, 1, 33–41.

Ghaziuddin, M. (2005) *Mental Health Aspects of Autism and Asperger Syndrome*. London: Jessica Kingsley Publishers.

Goodwin, D.W. (2000) *Alcoholism: The Facts*. Oxford: Oxford University Press.

Grandin, T. (2006) *Thinking in Pictures and Other Reports from My Life with Autism.* London: Bloomsbury.

Henault, I. (2006) *Asperger's Syndrome and Sexuality.* London: Jessica Kingsley Publishers.

Hendrickx, S. (2008) *Love, Sex and Relationships – What People with Asperger Syndrome Really Really Want.* London: Jessica Kingsley Publishers.

Hendrickx, S. and Newton, K. (2007) *Asperger Syndrome: A Love Story.* London: Jessica Kingsley Publishers.

Institute of Alcohol Studies (2006) *The Impact of Alcohol on the NHS.* London: Institute of Alcohol Studies. Available at www.ias.org.uk/resources/factsheets/nhs.pdf, accessed on 25 February 2008.

Mental health Foundation (2006) *Cheers? Understanding the Relationship between Alcohol and Mental Health.* London: Mental health Foundation.

Office for National Statistics (2006) *Alcohol Related Deaths.* General Register Office for Scotland, Northern Ireland Statistics and Research Agency. Available at www.statistics.gov.uk/cci/nugget.asp?id=1091, accessed on 23 March 2008.

Philippot, P., Kornreich, C., Blairy, S., Baert, I. *et al.* (1999) 'Alcoholics' Deficits in the Decoding of Emotional Facial Expression.' *Alcoholism: Clinical and Experimental Research 23,* 6, 1031–1038.

Royce, J.E. and Scratchley, D. (1996) *Alcoholism and Other Drug Problems.* London: Free Press.

Schneier, F.R., Blanco, C., Smita, A. and Liebowitz, M. (2002) 'The Social Anxiety Spectrum.' *The Psychiatric Clinics of North America 25,* 4, 757–774.

Schneier, F.R., Martin, L.Y., Liebowitz, M.R., Gorman, J.M. and Fyer, A.J. (1989) 'Alcohol abuse in social phobia.' *Journal of Anxiety Disorders 3,* 1, 15–23.

Slater-Walker, G. and Slater-Walker, C. (2003) *An Asperger Marriage.* London: Jessica Kingsley Publishers.

Stanford, A. (2003) *Asperger Syndrome and Long-Term Relationships.* London: Jessica Kingsley Publishers.

The Information Centre (2007) *Statistics on Alcohol: England 2007.* London: The Information Centre.

Thomas, S.E., Randall, C.L. and Carrigan, M.H. (2003) 'Drinking to Cope in Socially Anxious Individuals: A Controlled Study.' *Alcoholism: Clinical and Experimental Research 27,* 12, 1937–1943.

Uekermann, J., Channon, S., Winkel, K., Schlebusch, P. and Daum, I. (2007) 'Theory of mind, humour processing and executive functioning in alcoholism.' *Addiction 102,* 2, 232–240.

Uekermann, J., Daum, I., Schlebusch, P. and Trenckmann, U. (2005) 'Processing of affective stimuli in alcoholism.' *Cortex 41,* 2, 189–194.

Van Wijngaarden-Cremers, P.J.M. and van der Gaag, R.J. (2006) 'Addiction & Autism: Two sides of a same neurobiological coin?' Available at www.ditplb.or.id/2006/ppt/09h15%20Patricia%20van%20Wijngaarden-Cremers, accessed on 26 September 2007.

Young, R.M., Oei, T.P.S. and Knight, R.G. (1990) 'The Tension Reduction Hypothesis revisited: An alcohol expectancy perspective.' *British Journal of Addiction 85,* 31–40.

RESOURCES

Social anxiety information

Social Anxiety UK: www.social-anxiety.org.uk
Website for those with social anxiety or social phobia.

Asperger Syndrome and autism information

Asperger's Syndrome Foundation: www.aspergerfoundation.org.uk
London-based charity that organizes seminars and provides information for those with
Asperger Syndrome.

Aspire: www.aspire.bhci.org
Sussex, UK, based adult mentoring project which also provides training to organizations in
Sussex on AS awareness issues – Matt does volunteer work for the project. Only currently
supports those who live in Brighton and Hove. Available for consultancy in setting up
mentoring projects.

Hendrickx Associates: www.asperger-training.com
Sarah, Matt and another colleague deliver training courses and presentations for organizations
– universities, employers and service providers – and support for individuals, families and
partners affected by Asperger Syndrome and autism.

National Autistic Society: www.nas.org.uk
UK charity supporting those with autism.

Tony Attwood: www.tonyattwood.com.au
Considered to be the world authority on Asperger Syndrome and also a very nice man. Based
in Australia, but gives presentations worldwide.

Alcohol information

Addaction: www.addaction.org.uk

Alcohol Concern: www.alcoholconcern.org.uk

Alcoholics Anonymous: www.alcoholics-anonymous.org.uk

APPENDIX - THOUGHTS FROM FRIENDS AND FAMILY

Members of Matt's family and his first girlfriend (and close friend) were asked to share some of their thoughts and feelings about Matt and how they experienced him as a young man and his demise into alcoholism.

Matt's mum

One way in which Matt was different from his siblings was his clumsiness. He seemed to be always tripping over things, tripping up steps, spilling drinks and knocking things over. When Matt was on the move he tended to rush, and when he entered a room his father and I would often brace ourselves and wince, waiting for the inevitable crash.

Matt was a very bright child and he was always highly thought of at school, but he was often anxious; we called it highly strung. At school, the teachers were well aware of his ability and also that he sometimes found being at school stressful. Sometimes, when a teacher realized he was getting particularly worked up about something, he would be allowed to leave the classroom and go and sit in the school garden to 'cool off'.

Matt was a popular boy at school and friends were, and still are, very important to him, although he chose to be with friends that were special to him.

When Matt split from his first wife he returned home to live with his father and me. He didn't spend much time with us when he was in, preferring to be alone in his room, which suited us, as he was quite grumpy and morose company. Occasionally I would go to his room, perhaps to find something or put something away, and going in to the cupboards I would start to find empty alcohol cans and bottles stuffed in the oddest places, almost as if hidden. This prompted me to search the room further and I would find more under the bed, in fact in various places around the room, eventually retrieving enough to fill one or two black bin bags. More than anything this exasperated me, as I put it down to sheer laziness. I was not unduly worried, as I had no idea over how long these bottles and cans had accumulated. Each time this happened I complained to him about all this mess and told him to throw the bottles away as soon as they were empty, which he sheepishly agreed to do, but in fact never did. Although his father and I felt he may have been drinking rather heavily, there was a tacit agreement between all three of us that his drinking would never be mentioned as he seemed to function reasonably well, considering his recent split with his wife. Even though Matt's aunt was a recovering alcoholic, his father and I had no first-hand experience of this, and the idea that he had a drink problem was unthinkable.

It was not until Matt was with his second wife that I realized that his drinking was something to be more concerned about. Since the death of my husband I spent most weekends away from home at either of my children's homes. When I stayed with Matt and his wife the usual routine was that on Sunday morning Matt would go off to the pub when it opened and spend a few hours there drinking and reading the Sunday newspapers. He was never drunk when he returned but was often irritable. This was just accepted as part of Matt's nature. On one of these visits, not long after his fortieth birthday, Matt was out and his wife was talking about how lovely his birthday celebration had been, and about all the presents his friends had given him. The presents were nearly all bottles of alcohol and were stacked on top of a table. As his wife was chatting and picking up bottles at random to show me, she began to go silent as she saw that bottle after bottle had been opened, and most of the contents had gone. I could see that she was shocked as she realized that the alcohol he'd been given, which should have lasted for months, if not years, had disappeared in just a few weeks. She was upset by this discovery and was saying that this had to stop. I myself felt a great sense of unease and, for the first time, fear.

We are not a family that throws people out because of their behaviour or problems. There's too much love in the family for that to happen. Some people might say that this is where tough love is required, but in Matt's case there was knowledge that if he was thrown out it would probably kill him. We felt that he would not be able to cope on his own and survive.

This was because he seemed (and is still) a vulnerable person. An experience such as being thrown out would not have shaken him up and made him get his act together, he was incapable of this.

When he was so seriously ill I was desperate and just didn't know what to do. All I did know was that I felt powerless to do anything except keep him as safe as possible. Realizing he was so sick, I was frightened because he might die, but didn't know who to turn to. He desperately needed alcohol and when he had no money to buy any I would buy it for him, as the GP he was seeing at the time told him he should try slowly to cut down on his alcohol consumption, as stopping suddenly would be dangerous for him. This was the only advice that was offered. As Matt was also very depressed, on one visit to the GP's surgery we asked if he could be sectioned for his own safety and given a detox. The GP said that this was not possible, as he would have to have stopped drinking to prove his depression was not drink related. All of this seemed ludicrous. Matt couldn't cut down on his drinking; in fact, he seemed to be consuming more alcohol as the weeks went by. We couldn't get across how ill Matt was, or how desperate both he and we were about the whole situation. We left the surgery feeling nothing had been achieved, with the impression that the GP was a little bemused by these visits, especially when Matt preferred to sit on the floor instead of a chair.

When I look back at how ill Matt was and how close he came to death, I feel very angry at how little help and understanding was available to him from the medical profession. Nobody took our concerns seriously, and to them he was just another drunk whom we were indulging. This was not the case. He is very lucky to be alive today and we came very close to losing him.

Matt started drinking when he was eighteen years old, and looking back over the years, it is impossible to know the person he should have been. Since he has stopped drinking, he seems to be going through his lost youth and growing up as he should have done all those years ago. He has now become the person he truly is, which is better than we could have hoped for. I am constantly proud of him and am so pleased that he is managing his life and is now happy. He is doing a job he enjoys, making new friends and living by the sea, which has proved a wonderful therapy. I've realized that Matt is not a person to rest on his laurels. He takes full advantage of each day and makes things happen in his life. I feel the future for him now is full of exciting opportunities and possibilities that he will fully embrace. I wish him well.

Matt's sister, Mandy

To me, Matt was just my younger brother and at times, when he was quite young, we would play well together, but mostly Matt seemed happy to play on his own. From quite a young age he would periodically develop an interest in things that may or may not have been topical at the time: for instance, dinosaurs, many years before they became a craze of the population; Horatio Nelson and Nelson's Column; Tutankhamun; and the first lunar landing. When Matt was in the midst of one of his interests, my parents indulged him as far as was possible by providing him with facts and information about these, for although he didn't overtly pester for this, his suffering at being denied it was palpable.

Matt was very picky about the food he ate as a child, and would survive for months on end eating the same food every day. One meal I remember him insisting on having was luncheon meat and cucumber. Our mother couldn't persuade him to eat a meal with us, even on Christmas Day, as he much preferred eating on his own. I didn't think this too odd as a child, as I myself had food fads but I eventually grew out of these whereas Matt carried them over well into adulthood. He has since said that he found the ritual of sitting and eating together extremely stressful.

That Matt used alcohol to cope with the stress of life first emerged when he studied abroad for a year. On his return, he talked about how cheap the alcohol was to buy, and it was this that got him through. Matt settled back into life at home, and drinking on a daily basis became the norm for him. Although the family probably had some misgivings about this (for example, our parents had never been drinkers, much preferring a cup of tea as a cure all), his drinking was accepted, as he was able to lead a full life.

For me, however, the realization began to dawn that the sweet-natured, sensitive and sharp boy that Matt had once been was disappearing, to be replaced by an angry and quite bitter young man with a sarcastic tongue. At this point I didn't connect this change in him as being caused by his drinking, but felt sadly that this was the person into which he had matured. I also had a sense that his behaviour towards people, his lashing out, was a way of coping with all the things that happen in life, both stressful and mundane. I know my father recognized this also, for I can remember him saying often that life was all too much for Matt.

Over the years, I would visit Matt when he was with both his first and second wife. These visits often involved everyone drinking alcohol, and of course Matt always drank on these occasions. We would be drinking wine, and Matt would often top up with cans of extra-strong alcohol. It was difficult to say whether he was drinking too much, because he carried alcohol very well, never becoming outrageously drunk; but his ranting at life would become more malicious, interspersed with bitchy personal remarks.

When Matt visited me and my family, it was very hard work being with him. I found his anger and sniping draining even when it wasn't aimed at me. On one occasion, Matt had arranged to visit us early one evening so we could watch a film he had bought. My partner, Alex, and I were very tired and wanted to put our young children to bed, but they wanted to wait up to see Uncle Matt. The evening wore on with no sign of him, and I began to wish he wouldn't turn up. He arrived quite late, and although he had been drinking, he was by no means drunk. With no apology, he barged his way into our flat and plonked himself down on the floor in front of the television, calling for us to come and watch the film. I felt a mix of emotions, ranging from extreme anger to desolation, at what my brother had become. Alex was ready to blow, so I remained as calm as possible and gently chided Matt for being late. I could see that he was completely baffled by what I was saying, having no idea that his behaviour was unacceptable. He couldn't apologize, because as far as he was aware he had done nothing wrong; he just looked at me as if I was a cheerless person, devoid of all humour. We didn't watch the film, and Matt didn't stay long, as we insisted we were tired and needed to go to bed. When he had gone, Alex and I talked about what had happened. Alex was very angry, saying that Matt was hopeless and blaming his behaviour on the drink. I understood and trusted Alex's opinion, as he was extremely astute when it came to the subject of alcohol, himself having a drink problem, but to me it was more than just alcohol that was changing Matt. I realized that Matt had no idea how to be around people and what was an acceptable way to behave. His social skills were very poor – in fact, he had become graceless.

Although I knew for years before Matt's drinking reached crisis point that he had quite a problem, I didn't allow myself to dwell on this. I had problems in my own life, and years of living with an alcoholic, the father of my children, had caused me to put up barriers to what I felt unable to cope with.

However, it was Alex in whom I confided about Matt's drinking, as he was the person, in my opinion, most qualified to have any say in what was happening to Matt. On many occasions Alex would say that Matt would have to reach rock bottom before he would admit to himself that he was an alcoholic and seek help. Until it became obvious to other members of the family that things were going terribly wrong, it was difficult to talk to them about Matt's drinking, because they were in denial, the same as Matt.

In August 2003, Matt had been living with Mum for a few months since splitting from his second wife. During this time, he had been drinking heavily with one brief period of abstinence. One Saturday morning he approached Mum saying he didn't feel well and needed help. He was in very poor shape and must have been feeling very ill to have finally conceded that his alcohol consumption was the cause and was becoming a danger to him. Alex agreed to take him to the A & E department of the local hospital. We felt a terrific sense of relief that finally the admission of a problem had been made and that there would be professional people on hand to look after Matt and make him better. How naïve we were at that moment, and how little were we aware of the torturous months that lay ahead, though this started to become apparent before the day was over.

Alex stayed most of the day with Matt at A & E, but eventually in the evening returned home to leave Matt there on his own. Alex was totally drained and was unsure as to whether Matt would receive the help he needed. It was not until nearly midnight that Matt was able to phone us, and I thought he was going to say that all was well and he was on a hospital ward receiving a detox. Instead, he was on his own, waiting in the hospital grounds for a mini cab that was to take him to a psychiatric hospital located nearby. I was angry and afraid for him, knowing he was very vulnerable at that moment, and after having spent a gruelling day in hospital might decide that he was not yet ready to go further. I couldn't understand how casually the hospital was treating him, when the family knew that this first tentative step he had taken was a small miracle.

When Matt was discharged from the psychiatric hospital after his detox, we realized that treatment in a rehabilitation centre would not be available for him for many months. Even for him to receive regular counselling for alcoholism would take weeks to put in place. Inevitably, it was not long before Matt resumed drinking and quickly reinstated his pattern of consumption. As the weeks went on towards Christmas, we watched him drink ever larger amounts of alcohol and tried to reassure ourselves that if the medics didn't think his case was a matter of urgency then neither should we. This was very difficult to do, as each day was filled with constant low-grade anxiety and disbelief that somebody could drink so much and still function. We knew he was slowly dying as we were caught in a long drawn out waiting game. He became very thin and the whites of his eyes gradually turned a bright yellow, visual evidence of the damage his liver was sustaining. All we could do was support him as much as possible. Another detox might give his liver temporary respite, but in the long term was pointless unless followed up by immediate rehabilitation. Mum bore the brunt during this period and I feel sure (and Matt agrees) that if it wasn't for her immense love and understanding, her unstinting support and concern, he would have died.

By the time Christmas came, Matt was seriously ill but at least had started to receive alcohol counselling. Christmas was not anything the family could enjoy as only one thing occupied our minds: how much longer could Matt endure what was happening, and would he still be alive when rehabilitation became available?

Mum came to stay with me and my family on Christmas Eve, leaving Matt at her flat. On Christmas Day, Matt didn't feel up to coming over to visit, and towards the evening he phoned to say he had no alcohol at Mum's and hadn't had a drink for quite a few hours. Alex and I realized immediately how serious this was for him. It was fortunate that we had a big bottle of whisky at home, and Alex and I took it over to him, to stop the withdrawals he was suffering. Some people may question whether this was a wise thing to do. It was the only thing to do. Nothing else would have helped Matt at that moment. A trip to A & E would have achieved nothing. On Christmas night he would have been treated just the same as any other drunken person there. Who would have cared when we tried to explain he was having alcohol withdrawals, and how long would it have taken to make anyone understand that he needed immediate attention?

A few days later Matt came over to visit us. He was completely broken as a person and I can still visualize him sitting at the dining table, weeping quietly as Mum cuddled him. It was torture for him being with us, and it wasn't long before he wanted to leave to go back to Mum's place. When I said goodbye to him at the front door and watched him wander off into the night, I was filled with overwhelming sadness. He was so thin that the old black jacket he was wearing hung on him. His very demeanour revealed how desperately unhappy he was, and I prayed he would be alright and get back safely.

In January 2004, Matt had a routine blood test to guide the alcohol counselling he was receiving. The family was surprised when Matt wasn't contacted about the results. We believed Matt's liver had become seriously damaged and the blood test would reveal this, leading to some immediate action being taken to help him. We were very disappointed to hear nothing, and started to think that maybe we were over-dramatizing Matt's situation, and in fact it wasn't as serious as we believed. However, we had only to look at Matt to recognize that the seriousness of his illness was being overlooked by everyone in the medical profession entrusted with his well-being.

Two weeks later I went with Matt to his counselling session to offer support and to meet his counsellor. While we waited to be seen, Matt seemed uncomfortable and ill at ease. To a certain extent his frailty was disguised by the padded jacket he was wearing, but his face revealed all that was happening to his body. It was very thin and drawn, making his bright-yellow eyes appear larger than was normal for him and showing more clearly the anguish he was feeling. While sitting and making small talk, I had a sense of him fading before me as he no longer seemed a solid person. I couldn't wait to meet his counsellor, whom I felt sure would instantly see how much worse Matt had become. The counsellor was very welcoming, had a reassuring manner and didn't seem concerned over Matt's appearance. He told us that the blood test results still hadn't been received, and due to the lack of funding available to alcohol services, a detox followed by rehab was still many months away. Although I felt desperate, I calmly explained the family was very worried about the fact that

Matt was no longer eating, his eyes had become so yellow and he might die before rehab became available. I was told not to worry, as Matt wasn't really that ill and was getting some nourishment from the alcohol he was consuming. The yellowness of his eyes was explained away by some medical terms that I was barely listening to. All in all, it was explained, Matt had a long way to go before he was in any danger. I accepted this explanation, saying I hoped the counsellor was correct, but inside I felt immense rage and was screaming that he was mistaken and must be blind or stupid not see that Matt was dying. However, he hadn't yet received the results of the blood test.

The next day I received a phone call from Mum saying that Matt's counsellor was trying to contact me, as the blood test results had arrived and Matt needed to go to hospital. When the counsellor rang back, I took the phone call and immediately heard the urgency in his voice. Matt needed to be taken to A & E immediately, as enzyme levels in his liver were dangerously high. He reiterated that he had to be taken *immediately*, and that A & E would be expecting him. I was afraid, but also ecstatic that what the family had known for many months, that Matt was dying, was at last being acknowledged by the people who could help him.

After his first month in rehab, Matt was able to visit us and we were a little apprehensive about how things had been for him. The change in him was immediately obvious. He looked different, having cut his hair extremely short. He had put on a little weight and seemed so relaxed. As he described how his first month had been, I remember thinking that this was no longer the brother I had come to accept over those many difficult years. He spoke and responded differently. The impatience and irritation were no longer there, and he was actually interested in what we were saying. Both Mum and I enjoyed his company that weekend and missed him when he went back. We couldn't stop talking about him and agreed we were thrilled by the change in him. As the months went by, seeing Matt just got better. I looked forward to his visits, to laughing with him and confiding in him about things that were worrying me, something I had been unable to do before. He had many wise and encouraging things to say to me, things he'd learnt in rehab. All the love I felt for him, which had been buried during those awful years, returned.

Matt's discovery of the condition of Asperger Syndrome and recognition of this within himself was like winning first prize and was a truly exciting time for him. It has explained a lifetime of suffering and given him permission to be exactly who he is.

Today Matt is one of my favourite people to be with. We contact each other regularly and he is always kind, thoughtful and fun when we meet. He loves to help his family in whatever way he can, and I know if ever I'm in difficulties he will be there for me. My teenage daughters have had to learn about their Uncle Matt once again. When he was ill they told me they didn't like him and didn't want him to come over to see us. Now they seek him out, as he is very much on their wavelength and they end up having extremely random conversations with him. My youngest daughter particularly expresses how important Uncle Matt is to the family. Since the death of Alex she is very aware of the lack of a male presence in her life, and Matt being there helps to fill this space and give her a sense of security. His being around makes her feel safer.

I am so proud of Matt's achievement and am very aware that a lot of the time he has to be on guard as far as drinking is concerned. It would be very easy, seeing how well he is coping with life, to not appreciate the immense struggle he went through to be here today. This struggle, although on a lesser scale, continues each day for Matt and everything that has been gained would be lost, probably forever, should he have just one drink of alcohol.

Matt's first girlfriend, Jenny

When I first knew Matthew, when he was 19, he did not drink alcohol. That suited me as I was not much of a drinker either. We were both quite young and inexperienced for our years, with life ahead of us and, on the surface, few significant problems. Although we were going out together for about a year, I never really understood the depth of Matthew's anxieties and didn't know that he was using/had used tranquillizers. If I had been asked at the time, I would have said Matthew was quite happy-go-lucky. I couldn't, as it turned out, have been more wrong.

We have mostly kept in touch, and when Matthew was married to his second wife, I used to see them a reasonable amount. All of us who knew him were worried about his level of drinking at this point. He seemed unable to do anything if he hadn't had a lot of drink first, including hosting his 40th birthday party, which took place at my house. From being a humorous person, he had become argumentative and at times rude, seemingly unaware of the effect his words had on others. We were unaware of the full extent of his drinking, but could see the wear and tear it was causing his marriage. It was also evident that Matthew couldn't cope with changes in life and couldn't quite grow up. He didn't seem adult both in terms of his fear of responsibility and his seeming lack of awareness of the consequences of his own actions. However, when he was sober, there were flashes of the 'old' Matthew, of his inherent kindness and his humour.

I started to see a lot more of Matthew again once he returned to his mother's flat in 2002. He was drinking very heavily indeed; his appearance and health had deteriorated. He was, by turns, angry at the collapse of his marriage, deeply depressed with life and at a loss as to how to continue on into the future. He would not accept at this point that he was an alcoholic, although it was staring everyone who knew him in the face. We all told him, but at this point he just would not admit the truth. Over a period of about a year, and an abortive attempt to stop drinking, Matthew's mental and physical health deteriorated further. We were all worried about him, but found it difficult to know how to help. I would listen and offer suggestions, but I also knew that they would do no good unless Matthew acknowledged the depths of his problems and wanted to do something about them himself. I was aware that he might die, but it seemed as if he would not pull back from the brink. I have since learnt that it is common for alcoholics to have to reach rock bottom before treatment can work. So it proved with Matthew. It was only his near experience of death, the knowledge that he really would die if he drank again, and the tireless efforts of his mum and sister to find help for him, that mean he is still alive today.

I saw Matthew very regularly throughout his rehabilitation and heard a lot about the Cognitive Behavioural Therapy he experienced. It was fascinating and heartening watching him accept that he was an alcoholic, and then realize that he could stop being one. It really was encouraging to see how Matthew 'grew up'. He acquired a lot more self-knowledge and came to accept a lot more things about his nature. A great part of this was his discovery that he is on the Autistic Spectrum, what that means for him, and how to live with it. I remember talking to him shortly after he had seen a programme on Asperger's Syndrome, and his confidence that most of the 'Asperger traits' applied to him. When I first heard this I was sceptical, because in many ways Matthew is more able to function than other people I know who are autistic. However, I soon realized that what I had always thought of as his 'unusual brain' was probably a form of autism. Matthew's journey to diagnosis was very important to him and, in my opinion, is closely linked to the success he has had in overcoming alcoholism. I think it would have been much harder for him to get and stay clean had he not undergone this journey towards self-discovery.

Seeing Matthew now is fantastic. He really is a changed man. He takes pleasure in the small things in life. He is self-aware, and lives well with that awareness.

INDEX